Praise for Murray Bay

"Judy Carmack Bross has recreated the hauntingly pleasurable world of Murray Bay, Quebec, where Sedgwicks of Massachusetts and Ohio's Tafts were among the American aristocrats maintaining summer estates at the turn of the last century. Her evocative descriptions of scenery, domestic architecture, costumes, and even mannerisms and vernacular, provide a fresh summer breeze from the past to sweep away the years and transport the reader on a Gilded Age holiday."

Megan McKinney, author
The Magnificent Medills

"What you and the book discover and evoke is what is clearly an amazing place through a tapestry of extraordinary lives which may have vacationed in Murray Bay, but also defined a century. From your book, Murray Bay emerges as a mystical place where all is possible–where tradition and progressive ideas, art and history, past and future co-exist. It's intimate and grand–perhaps Murray Bay just has too much oxygen. It's the story of a small beautiful place in Quebec, but also the story of a people who are the North American continent. It has the making of a great epic film–one, I fear, that would be very expensive to make–and I don't know a big enough filmmaker to make it."

Milos Stehlik,
Founder/Executive Director
Facets Multi-Media.

More Praise for Murray Bay

"Judy Carmack Bross has done a masterful job researching a subject dear to her heart, and her writing will make you feel present among North American aristocracy over a hundred years ago, not wanting to ever leave. Reading Murray Bay magically transports you to an enchanting place during a magnificent time in history."

A.P. Greenwood, Author
Judy Bross' High School classmate

"Judy Carmack Bross's parents, George and Bonnie Carmack, were prolific, eminent journalists adept for the exacting word and true emotion. Now comes Judy to embellish the family writerly escutcheon with her admirable, charming *Murray Bay*, an incisive adventure into Turn-of-the-Century nostalgia that illuminates the quaint Canadian summer resort of America's wealthy and beautiful celebrities.

Judy's magnificent research unearths Murray Bay not only for vibrant history but the eccentricities of the rich and famous from their titillating, startling behavior down to the mundane. In their pink, blue and even yellow fabulous "cottages" where they changed clothes six times a day, they threatened dinner guests with sharp knives, conducted secret scandalous love affairs, and even noted the murder of a beautiful painter which went unsolved.

Murray Bay tugs at the Edith Wharton mystique, scattering a plethora of statesmen, millionaires, authors, artists, and 'the most beautiful women in the world.' The well-traveled author calls Murray Bay the geographical love of her life and proves it with her pen."

Vance Trimble, author
Pulitzer Prize winner

More Praise for Murray Bay

"I am stunned by the knowledge Judy Carmack Bross has expressed. I feel as though I've been transported through a different portal of memory. Most of my personal memories of Murray Bay have been physical— hiking, fishing, exploring, and interacting with people. The author's portal is through the social associations and reminiscences. Most of the names of people were familiar, but faint, and yet I can now recollect vague stories told by my mother over the years. I was drawn by the stories of many of the well-to-do families who were early to arrive in Charlevoix. Having gone to school near Newport, RI, I was almost embarrassed by the wealth displayed by the "summer cottages" there. Those who chose to be in Murray Bay certainly lived a good life but they expressed it in a far different way; they seemed to be more interested in the physical activities and simply being in Murray Bay. The houses were elegant in their simplicity but not quite so showy as Newport.

In the words of Tim Porteous, a childhood friend, 'Murray Bay, like Nirvana, is not so much a place as a state of mind; the difficulty is not to locate it, but to attain it. It is not that there is a deliberate conspiracy to exclude the casual visitors, but rather that a web of interlocking friendships and shared pleasures connects the regulars, and there is no prescribable method for becoming enmeshed.' I'm sure that we all have our own keys that bind us to this very special place. I know that it has been difficult to explain my attraction to Charlevoix, as an American, to my Quebec friends."

Tommy Hoopes
Murray Bay historian/collector

MURRAY BAY

THE GILDED AGE SUMMER RESORT OF
TAFTS, SEDGWICKS, BLAKES, MINTURNS,
AND THEIR FRIENDS

Judy Carmack Bross

Judy Carmack Bross

COPYRIGHT

ISBN-13: 978-1511647922
ISBN-10: 1511647922
Library of Congress Control Number 2015906157

Published in the United States of America

Front cover photograph
Fonds Roland Gagné
Musée de Charlevoix collection

Back cover portrait
Edith Minturn Phelps Stokes
Artist Cecelia Beaux
Private collection

Inside Title Page
Murray Bay Protestant Church
Musée de Charlevoix collection

TABLE OF CONTENTS

Judy Carmack Bross

DEDICATION

This book is dedicated to my husband, John Bross, in recognition of his devotion to the Murray Bay Protestant Church, and to our friend, Sebastien Tremblay, who represents the exemplary nature of Murray Bay habitants.

I have wandered over a good part of the inhabited world. I have seen many places, and some I have loved and love still. But I know of no other spot that I love as I love this little village of Pointe au Pic and the country that surrounds it. I know of no group of people for whom I have a deeper respect or a more lasting affection than I feel toward those French Canadians whom we call the "habitants."

John Rathbone Oliver
"Foursquare"1929

INTRODUCTION

"The air of Murray Bay is as intoxicating as champagne, yet without the hangover."
                    —President William Howard Taft

Newport, Jekyll Island, Bar Harbor, Lenox–all glittering summer destinations during America's Gilded Age of opulence in the early 1900s. Visited only for a few weeks each year in their heyday by Vanderbilts, Astors, Fishes, and other members of the American aristocracy, their homes remain as rambling renaissance palaces with the stories of their greater days left for only tour guides to tell.

But the ghosts of the Gilded Age remain in Murray Bay, Quebec, Canada which, like Brigadoon, can't be found on a map. William Howard Taft, American "royalty"—the Minturns, Sedgwicks, Tiffanys and Vanderbilts, Canadian dynasties like the Blakes, who helped build the new Canada—to them, summer meant spending at least three months in graceful clapboard villas on the St. Lawrence River. Many of their houses remain on what is simply called "the Boulevard" facing the purple-toned Laurentian Mountains and capes high above the wide river.

Many descendants of those who came to Murray Bay at the turn of the last century remain to tell the tale. Days filled with picnics, fishing, tennis, and lawn parties ended with white tie dinners along the Boulevard in villas framed by graceful verandas, not at all fitting the definition of a "cottage." Highest government officials from both the United States and Canada mingled with visiting Russian royalty, New York socialites, and internationally famous authors and movie actresses. In Murray Bay, you did not miss a minute and you often changed clothes six times a day.

Lady Evelyn Grey

Lady Evelyn Grey and friend

Lady Evelyn Grey, daughter of Albert Henry George Grey, the 4th Earl Grey and Governor General of Canada, suns on the beach close to the Murray Bay Protestant Church and paints the capes with a friend, both frequent activities of visitors.

"It attracts me just because it's hard to get to and because the few people who go there love it so much that they want to keep others away," said Mrs. J. Barton Randolph, in Rock and Sand, the iconic Murray Bay novel by John Rathbone Oliver, published in 1930.

By 1910, when we pick up its story, Murray Bay was still hard to reach but oh, the intriguing people who found it!

Mrs. de Guilhaus, Mrs. Sanford, Mrs. Dixon
Musée de Charlevoix

Judy Carmack Bross

CHAPTER ONE

A Summer Sunday in Murray Bay

"The most beautiful words in the English
language are summer afternoon..."
—Henry James to Edith Wharton.

Deceptively simple except for overflowing bouquets of delphinium and sweet peas blossoming for that day's celebration, the little Murray Bay Protestant Church beside the wide St. Lawrence River summoned with its pealing bell the patrician and the powerful of the United States and Canada. It was August 20, 1910, the height of the Gilded Age in a summer colony like no other. Glorious sunshine reflected off the river and the elegant summer homes—forever known as "cottages"—seemed to look down from the Boulevard above the small church in approval.

How could you pick the most beautiful woman in the church? Was it the swanlike elegance of the fashionable Edith Minturn Phelps Stokes who sat beside her aristocratic architect husband, Newton Phelps Stokes, or the Minturn blue eyes or the regal bearing of her sister, Sarah May Sedgwick

1

that would capture your attention? Could it be the merry Rose Tiffany or the little six year-old blonde, Rosamond Pinchot, whispering with her cousins, who would one day be called "the loveliest woman in America?"

You could make a definite case that Edith would be the most unforgettable. Two of the Fin de Siècle's most famous artists would count Edith among their masterpieces, the directness and insouciance of her stare capturing attention for 100 years and counting. John Singer Sargent proclaimed her the first modern woman when he directed her to pose in casual clothes for his painting which now hangs in the Metropolitan Museum of Art and Daniel Chester French chose her as the model for the Statue of the Republic, the 80-foot golden lady which became the focal point of the 1893 World's Columbian Exposition in Chicago. At Chicago's Field Museum in 2013, a glittering gala transformed the main exhibition hall into the fair's midway with images of Edith as the golden lady all around the room, an icon for an event that raised over $2 million. Postcards and posters of Sargent's painting have never stopped selling at museum gift shops around the world.

Seated with Edith, Gertrude, and their children that Sunday would be their eldest sister, May, and her patrician husband, Henry Dwight Sedgwick, with their three children. The fourth Minturn sister, Mildred Scott, the only one to graduate from college (Bryn Mawr, 1897), would be in Paris, touring the city with her best friends, the Bertrand Russells. Together they were considered classical beauties by many discerning observers of society.

Their mother encouraged a European tour for the wisdom it would bring and one person mistook the four Minturn sisters, tall and with perfect carriage, as "four Russian princesses" exploring Italy. Each of the sisters would one day be the subject of a delicious book, either about their own particular brand of fascination or that of their descendants.

The gentleman with the most commanding presence in the church would have for the past seventeen years been William Howard Taft, not only for his girth, but also for his place at the head of a large family. However, in 1910, he would not have been in Murray Bay because he was serving as the 27th President of the United States and believed that a sitting President should not leave the country. He would have been at the summer White House in Beverly, Massachusetts. His favored seats on the front two side rows, where he would return following his Presidency, were filled with other Tafts whose descendants included governors of Rhode Island and Ohio, two U.S. Senators and Congressmen, and three cabinet members. A large brass plaque in the church commemorates when the president sat.

The Taft family in Murray Bay
Musée de Charlevoix collection

U.S. Supreme Court Justice Harlan stood stately and erect in the center with his family that day, as he did each Sunday, but William Hume Blake, fisherman, storyteller, and perhaps Quebec's most fascinating character would have captured your imagination by the French Canadian touches in his clothing. Helen Taft Manning, the president's daughter, said that "[h]e knew more about French Canada, fishing, camping out and writing about than any other person in the world." He often wore his fishing hat to church.

Manning would have added that the wealthiest man in the church was George Bonner, "who made his money in the New York Stock Exchange and bought the whole waterfront property east of the church."

Seated close to his friend Bonner would be Alfred Chapin, a wealthy New Yorker and former Mayor of Brooklyn, whose daughter Grace would marry Hamilton Fish. The family would serve for nearly a century in the United States Congress with great influence.

The gentleman who would have been judged the most exquisitely dressed would be Henry Dwight Sedgwick, known as "Harry" to his friends and "Babbo" to his family, a noted writer and master gardener. The title of his book, *The Epicurean*, one of over 35 books he published, said it all about his refined nature. Married to Edith Minturn's oldest sister, May, his passionate scholarship ranged from Renaissance Italy to eighteenth century France. Everyone agreed that he exhibited the Sedgwick male family attribute: *Charm.*

Members of the most illustrious groups of patrician families—Minturns, Blakes, Sedgwicks, Tafts, Fishs, Cabots, McCaggs, and Harlans—had greeted each other with enthusiasm, even though they had dined together the night before in exquisite formal attire seemingly incongruous in their rural surroundings. Unlike house parties described by Edith Wharton and other chroniclers of Golden Age house parties where guests didn't arrive until noon and played bridge well into the night, Murray Bay provided days where members of the summer community never missed a picnic on the beach, golf at the club, bazaars, square dancing with accordion and harmonica music provided by local musicians, and white tie dinners along the Boulevard.

Two families in the room would have spent previous summers in the Berkshires, close to the residence of Edith Wharton who chronicled the Gilded Age. Isaac Newton Phelps Stokes' father, Anson, had built a Tudor mansion in Lenox. With its 100 bedrooms, at that time it was believed to be the largest residence in the country. It was where he initiated his courtship of Edith Minturn.

Several families were among the old aristocracy of New York and had spent endless summers abroad since childhood. Some had danced at the grand balls of Newport, hunted at Jekyll Island, and lived in the mansion that would be part of the Morgan Library today; but Murray Bay would be their champagne—the place they would hold in their hearts forever.

In perhaps her most perceptive social chronicling of the Gilded Age, *The Age of Innocence*, Edith Wharton had written of "the tight little citadel of New York." In Murray Bay, they would meet not only their peers, but the privileged of Canada as well. It would be the Blake family of Toronto who issued the most prized invitation to tea, whether at their most famous home, Maison Rouge, or several others up and down the Boulevard.

A granddaughter of Cornelius Vanderbilt built what would be known as the "blue cottage" which was subsequently owned by the Culver family whose son, David Culver, headed Alcan, the Canadian Mining company and aluminum manufacturer. The Blue Cottage was part of a color trio—blue, pink, and yellow—of spacious villas which included the equally famous Yellow Cottage, still a sparkling sunburst, beautifully maintained by a Washington, D.C. family. The Pink Cottage, owned by World War I hero, Hume Blake, was destroyed by fire in 1932, making way for one of the most beautiful homes in the area—Les Falaises, a Norman chateau.

Even the children in the church on that day in 1910, in some cases would one day be recognized for their glamour, notoriety, heroic sacrifice, or athletic fame. Rosamond Pinchot, the six year-old blonde with saucer blue eyes and pouty lips, sitting beside her mother, Gertrude Minturn Pinchot, seventeen years later would be called by the British poet, Iris Tree, "the loveliest woman in America." She had been swept into a stage and film career, her great beauty spied on the luxury liner, *The Aquitania* by the impresario Max Reinhardt.

At age nine, Harriet Camac, already captivating with large blue eyes, would one day be painted by a European artist in a series called "The most beautiful women in America." The daughter of wealthy doctor, Charles Camac, Harriet would carry the secret of a handsome pilot, their love affair, and a little girl, to her grave to be discovered by another summer resident who found her letters almost 100 years later.

Harriet Camac
Maryse Cote collection

The most colorful boy in the church would be the 12-year old, who always wore a kilt of the distinctive yellow and red Buchanan plaid to church. When he grew up, he would build at least four grand summer cottages on the hilltop road nearby, famous among the privileged as "the Boulevard."

The two Sedgwick sons, Francis and Minturn, for the rest of their lives would be the most handsome men in any room. Minturn, a Harvard football legend, led Harvard to win the 1920 Rose Bowl against Oregon. He would marry Helen Peabody, daughter of Groton School's Founder and Headmaster, Endicott Peabody, who often spent part of his summer in Murray Bay. Minturn's brother, Francis, fathered seven children, including Edie Sedgwick, the beautiful, but ill-fated Andy Warhol star, named for her great aunt, Edith Minturn Phelps Stokes. Edith's own daughter, Helen, had been adopted in England in 1906 and would forever cherish Murray Bay visits with her attractive cousins.

The Blake and Wrong cousins sat close by with their families. The life of the handsome red-haired Harold Wrong, age nineteen in 1910, would be cut tragically short. The son of noted Canadian historian, George McKinnon Wrong, of Toronto, who served as an usher that day, Harold was an Oxford University student. He read the news of the outbreak of the First World War while visiting in Murray Bay and nearby Cap a l'Aigle and enlisted. Just 25 years old when he died, he wrote poems recently compared to those of the poet, Rupert Brooke. Sitting beside him would have been his 18-year old cousin, Gerald Blake, grandson of the former Premier of Ontario, who died with his cousin at the battle of the Somme. Gerald's letters from the front to a fiancée he would never see again were recently published by the great-granddaughter of his young love.

From the windows of the Murray Bay Protestant Church, parishioners could look out upon the broad and frequently rough St. Lawrence River that dominates the Charlevoix region in the province of Quebec. Two and a half centuries before, Samuel de Champlain had sailed into the bay before heading forward to discover Quebec. A cartographer and a botanist, Champlain came close to shore along the St. Lawrence, cataloging plants that appeared similar to ones in his native France. Champlain named the spot "Malle Baye" because the harbor would literally dry up at low tide and he was unable to land.

Many of the settlers were Scottish soldiers who served in the army of General Wolfe during the British conquest of Quebec in 1759. When their regiments disbanded, they decided to stay in the area and married French-speaking settlers whose descendants still bear such Scottish names as McNicholl, Frazier, and Warren.

The town of Pointe au Pic would grow up around the dock where the large wooden paddle wheelers called "bateaux blancs" brought up summer dwellers and their guests from Montreal and points beyond. When a cholera epidemic swept through the big cities in 1830, panic translated into the determination to escape to the country. The first ship to make the run from Montreal was the *Waterloo* of the St. Lawrence Steamboat Company, followed by the Montreal & Quebec Steamship Company which made runs twice a week to Pointe au Pic with two ships, the *Alliance* and the *Rowland Hill*.

Although many of the guests came to Montreal or Quebec City by train, the Transcontinental Railway wasn't extended to Murray Bay until the following summer, July 1911. Only a dirt road connected Quebec City and Murray Bay in 1910 and a single lane road existed until the 1960s when the road widened and several of the town's most beautiful villas were torn down. To most, it was a hard journey all in all, but well worth it for those who arrived in June and stayed until October.

The flag of Charlevoix features colors that say it all: green for the forests, its forests for hiking and picnicking, bright yellow for *soleil*, its sunshine like no other because of the freshness of the air in this northern clime, and blue for the *fleuve*, the wide St. Lawrence River, half saltwater and half fresh when it reached Murray Bay, and streams filled with pink trout for fishing.

Historian George Wrong, seated with his son Harold that August day, wrote amusingly in *A Canadian Manor and its Seigneurs*, 1908, of the calèches that waited at the long Murray Bay dock for the summer residents, eager to be ferried up the steep hill to their cottages.

"It comes from Old France, a two-wheeled vehicle, with a seat hung on a stout leather strap, running from front to back on each side of a wooden frame. It is not a vehicle for those sensitive to slight jolts. The driver sits in a tiny seat in front and one is amazed at the agility with which even old men spring from this perch to walk up and down steep hills. Their ponies are beautiful little animals, especially fitted by a long development for work in this hilly country. So well do they mount its heights that travellers repeat an unconfirmed tradition that they have been known to climb trees."

Passengers alighting from calèche
Musée de Charlevoix collection

Land to build the church was given to a small group of English-speaking Protestants in 1866 by descendants of the Scotsman John Nairne, one of two Seigneurs of the area who had received Seigneuries from the new British government. The Seigneuries were originally given to prominent individuals by the French crown who were expected to develop the land and farm it, as well as attract colonists.

Hubert Warren, described as a navigator and carpenter, agreed to construct the church for the price of $400, with sashes, doors, and other extras to cost an additional $225. The church's original size was fifty feet by thirty feet with a chancel fifteen feet wide and eight feet deep. The church was finished in 1867, the year of Canada's birth, when Upper and Lower Canada were united, an auspicious beginning for both country and church.

13

In 1902, the chancel was enlarged. Hubert Warren's nephew, Charles Warren, the legendary architect of the region who created the "cottages" where so many of the Charlevoix celebrities lived in the golden age of Murray Bay and still do today, carried out the changes to the little church which brought together so many of the people that day in 1910. President Taft, Justice Harlan, and the Minturn family were among the generous donors.

Charles Warren's assignment was to clad the church in stone using architectural plans donated by Edith's husband, Newton Phelps Stokes, and the Phelps Stokes family would have come up from New York to celebrate the conclusion of the project on this bright August day of 1910.

Murray Bay Protestant Church being clad in stone.
Musée de Charlevoix collection

Fifteen years before, Edith and Phelps Stokes had been married in the little church. The seven bridesmaids wore pink dresses and straw hats decorated with sweet peas and snapdragons from her mother's garden facing the river. Edith's dress with full sleeves and a long train, emphasized her regal bearing as did the statue of her as the golden lady for the World's Fair of 1893.

Due to a sudden rain shower, a calèche had ferried the wedding party the short distance across the street to the little church. After an extended Parisian honey-moon, Mr. and Mrs. Isaac Newton Phelps Stokes had sat for John Singer Sargent in London, where perhaps the most famous of his paintings would capture her spirit.

That day in 1910, bright summer light filtered through clear glass windows over the entrance. It would be four years before Rose Tiffany, daughter-in-law of Charles Tiffany, would make possible the donation of Pink Art Nouveau windows honoring Parishioner Jones Beach. Rose Healy Tiffany also would have been among the beauties at church that day. Her own home, called *La Folie Rose*, was given to her by her father-in-law and stood at the top of a high hill overlooking the church on the Boulevard des Falaises. Like Rose Tiffany's *La Folie Rose*, Americans and English-speaking Canadians (Anglophones) chose French names for their villas—*Bord de L'Eau*, *Le Barachois*, *Les*

Cerceaux. Someone once said that French was sprinkled like salad dressing by many of the fashionable of that era who once would have learned it in school or in travels on the continent. A few homes, such as those of the Harlans, both Justices of the United States Supreme Court, had Scottish names, such as Braemead. Another Scottish homeowner on nearby Cote Pednaud chose the name "Brandy Hill."

The pews in the little church by the wide St. Lawrence, described with reverence by the French Canadians as *Le Fleuve*, were filled not only with Americans, but also with influential and elite Canadians who led that country in its times of glory and expansion. Samuel Hume Blake, father of the famous fisherman, William Hume Blake, had been Chancellor of Upper Canada and was a leader of the Confederation Movement with united Upper and Lower Canada in 1867, and historian George MacKinnon Wrong wrote compelling histories of the nation.

Murray Bay attracted the select and the famous. At first, some rented from local "habitants" happy to open their homes for extra revenue or they stayed in hotels such as Chamard's Lorne House and eventually the Manoir Richelieu. Community descriptions were shared reverentially. You didn't tell just anyone and being a hard destination to reach helped keep that exclusivity.

Murray Bay was where Mary Todd Lincoln came for solitude in 1873 and signed the guest register at the Hotel Duberger. Others claim that she stayed at the Riverside Hotel; perhaps she also stayed there as well. The very few who saw Mary Lincoln on this solitary visit said that she spoke perfect French.

Murray Bay's summer residents seemed to know everyone. According to Christian Harvey of the Histoire de Charlevoix, Saint-Exupery drew his inspiration for Le Petit Prince from his friend Charles de Konick whose family owned *Les Croutes*, one of the two log cabins on the Boulevard. Several cottage owners entertained the Russian Prince Grigor Galitzin when he visited Murray Bay in 1884.

Murray Bay combined the magic of sunshine and fresh air contrasting with heat and possible pandemics in big cities and the exotic fascination of the French Canadian culture with inexpensive land and labor to become a Gilded Age destination. Activities such as golf, tennis, picnics, and hiking in the Laurentian foothills invigorated visitors from June through October. Trout fishing on the nearby Murray River or at exclusive fishing camps where local guides cooked your catch was legendary. Dancing, especially the Virginia Reel, which was accompanied by French Canadian music, was done for the fun of it, with William Howard Taft known as the best dancer of all.

Meats and vegetables grown at farms nearby were delivered, along with ice, to the large houses that soon lined the hills behind the wharves. Families often went out in rowboats or canoes with tea baskets for an afternoon picnic on a nearby beach, building fires to heat their kettles.

Each summer Micmac Indians would sell woven willow baskets beneath the cliffs at the dock to the women who came back each summer, as well as passengers from the bateaux blanches which stopped briefly on their way to Taddoussac farther east or Cacouna across the river. A bazaar to benefit the Red Cross, the American branch headed by summer resident Mabel Boardman, was held on a mid-summer's afternoon at the Murray Bay Golf Club, the fourth oldest golf club in North America, second oldest in Canada that have been continually played in the same place. Ladies dressed in gauzy embroidered white dresses bolstered by frilly petticoats and hats to rival today's Ascot's opening day wandered amidst elaborate arches of flowers and pine branches spotlighting tea tables and bountiful handmade goods for sale. Local artists sold portfolios of their works and great collections of significant paintings began.

Red Cross Bazaar
Musee de Charlevoix collection.

In 1918, pioneer travel writer Antonia Stemple glowingly described Murray Bay handicrafts. Summer residents would have decorated rooms with tufted or braided rugs, linens, and bed coverings, so different from the heavy Victorian brocades found in their New York mansions and, to Ms. Stemple, what a difference these native fabrics made.

"It is in Murray Bay among the French habitants and the Indians—and the two often intermarry—that one finds one of the most unique and distinctive handicrafts in the country, with the love of color and design producing very meritorious and artistic work."

She writes, "The wool for the blankets is spun and woven by the women at hand wheels and looms, dyed with their own vegetable dyes, and

19

there is never an eye on the clock. The blankets are very light, but of pure wool, hence very warm. They wear and wear and stand hard service. Geometric and conventional designs are used for the most part and it is seldom that you see two exactly alike.

"The bedspreads and coverlets are equally distinctive and possibly more beautiful. They are of hand-spun linen, sometimes of natural color, and again of white, blue or pink. They have either tufted designs, or patterns darned in with colored wool called boutinee. Prim little pine and fir trees, tiny conventionalized houses, and animals are the principal motifs in the designs and often a spread will tell a story to the discerning."

A typical living room: Le Caprice
Courtesy of Elisabeth Bacque

Ms. Stemple, who wrote for "Good Housekeeping" couldn't resist adding her impresssions of the overall magic of Murray Bay.

"Some of the most magnificent summer residences on the continent are to be found among the heavily wooded mountains overlooking the broad St. Lawrence, but when the steamer docks at the long wharf and you have your first glimpse of Pointe-au-Pic, as the old French-Canadian settlement straggling along the river front is called, you would not dream that a little farther back are hotels and residences which vie in elegance with those of Newport."

Quai de Pointe-Au-Pic
Musèe de Charlevoix collection

The smell of cedar was everywhere, even from the breezy verandas where summer residents gathered in the late afternoons to look northwards as the Laurentian Mountains turned lavender blue as the skies turned pink. In his *Memoirs of an*

Epicurean, Henry Dwight Sedgwick describes even the mud flats at low tide where the Murray River meets the St. Lawrence near the church cape as magnificent. "[w]hen the rising or the setting sun kisses them with golden alchemy, they shimmer and blush and colour, and, as Cinderella dropped the rags she sat in by the kitchen fire to put on the ball gown that won the prince's heart, clothe themselves and glow, rose-tinted flats and sparkling pools, in beauty."

While on local picnics on inland lakes, summer visitors would marvel at moose observed from a distance or catch glimpses of foxes, the color of a maple leaf in fall. An early travel writer Gordon Brinley wrote in *Away to Quebec,* "Looking from a wide windowed dining room of my hotel in this enchanting place made me intimately acquainted with an egret, a hairy marmot, a downy woodpecker and a jaeger which looked like a very large seagull."

William Hume Blake, one of the world's most recognized outdoors authors wrote, "The weather of Murray Bay has played a major part in drawing people thither: air indescribably fresh and stimulating, the assurance of coolness when all the west and south wilts and gasps; these gifts, with the river and the everlasting hills, no meddling hand may spoil…"

"The Boulevard of cottages"
Musee de Charlevoix collection

Although many were designed by world-class and high-end architects such as Stanford White and Charles McKim of perhaps the most prestigious architectural firm at the time, the houses were forever referred to as "cottages."

Charles Warren, the church's architect in 1910, became the major architect of Murray Bay. Warren, who grew up in Murray Bay, had studied in Boston and worked on early Murray Bay villas with White, McKim, and Phelps Stokes.

Tommy Hoopes, a New Hampshire resident who has summered all his life in Murray Bay, is the local resident who best channels Charles Warren. Tommy's parents and other relatives experienced the golden era of Murray Bay from their Charles

Warren house high on the Boulevard and Tommy is restoring their home according to Warren's specifications.

Tommy Hoopes relates that Warren would meet with a family at the end of a summer, explore their newly purchased property, offer tall ladders to experience a second-floor look because a view of the river is everything, and then send them off to their boats with the promise to create their dream house over the winter. When the family returned the following June, he would have built the house, added all the furnishings down to the last embroidered placemat, filled it with lilacs and peonies, and presented the keys to the new owners.

In April of 1910, Halley's comet streaked across the skies. Mark Twain, born when that comet had last been seen and who predicted he would die when it was seen again, died the day after the comet returned. Florence Nightingale, legendary nurse of the Crimea, had died just days before. Mother Teresa, the woman who duplicated her courage, was born. George V became King of England upon the death that year of his father Edward VII. Wilhelm II was King of Germany and Armand Fallieres was President of France.

On May 21st, 20,000 people came together in New York's Union Square to view a Suffragette demonstration although the 19th Amendment giving women the right to vote wouldn't be passed until 1910. William D. Boyce founded the Boy Scouts in the United States and William Howard Taft started the presidential tradition of throwing out the first baseball of the season, although his mind quite possibly was on his friends and family in Murray Bay.

Foreign spies, highly placed Canadian diplomats, Andy Warhol Factory Girls like Edie Sedgwick and Brigit Berlin who summered in Murray Bay, and large groups of garden enthusiasts from around the world descending on Frank and Anne Cabot's Quatre Vents, (considered by many to be the finest garden in North America) would be part of Murray Bay's intriguing future later in the century and subjects for a sequel, "Mid-Century Murray Bay."

In 1910, the women dressed for church in long white lawn dresses with wide summer straw hats festooned with flowers and artfully arranged ribbons. Both women and men often changed clothes five or six times a day in Murray Bay. Even today, after church, a traditional luncheon at a fellow parishioner's villa is preceded by sherry on the piazza. Couples change for golf, a hike, or play practice, and then dress formally for dinner at home surrounded by guests and glittering crystal and silver. Children of all ages had their own events together, with the older ones looking after the others, anticipating games by the Trou, a large pool in front of a waterfall near a delightful sandy beach on the Murray River, and as they got older, perhaps time spent listening to French Canadian songs by the firelight along the River.

Church was about to begin and the little structure, which held about fifty people in 1910, would be filled with people there to celebrate the completion of the church's new coat of stone. The little church would have services only during the summer for the Americans and Anglo Canadians, offering both Anglican (the Canadian equivalent of the American Episcopal Church) and Presbyterian services on the same day. The summer colony was almost totally Protestant in a Catholic and French region. The Murray Bay Protestant Church had become not only the site for Sunday services and strong Sunday School instruction for children, it also served as the cultural center in the days before a museum and concert center were built. Although we do not know for sure that all we describe were present that day due to unexpected travel or illness, each would have been expected to attend due to the significance of the celebration and the importance of the church as a social, as well as a religious institution.

Although church records telling who led the services began only in 1912, the minister would likely have been Reverend G.R. Fothergill from

Quebec. In 1908, he had been a missionary to the Trans-Continental Railroad of Canada, investigating poor conditions for its workers, but spending the summer among the Murray Bay congregation was something he did for many years.

Alexander McKay, a legendary Scotsman and dedicated sportsman for whom the sacristy is dedicated, was the church's most famous early preacher. Educated in Edinburgh and London, he sailed to Montreal in 1879 and retreated to Murray Bay because of poor health conditions in that city. He loved fishing expeditions along the St. Lawrence. He died in 1901 at Sept Iles, a remote destination on the north shore discovered by Jacques Cartier in 1535 and by Basque fishermen. The cause of death was eating tainted mussels.

It is almost a certainty that the flowers on the altar would have come from the Frederick Law Olmsted garden of Therese Davis McCagg, widow of the Chicago millionaire Ezra McCagg who, for many years was the church's most loyal volunteer. Mrs. McCagg often sat with her friend, Mabel Boardman, head of the American Red Cross, owner of one of the largest Murray Bay cottages which she called "Mooring Lights" since it stood high on the Boulevard with an uninterrupted view of the ships along the St. Lawrence. Miss Boardman, who never married, took over the Red Cross from Clara

Barton and would supervise Red Cross efforts to help survivors of the luxury ocean liner *Titanic* that would sink two years later in 1912. Murray Bay was known for its strong women like Theresa McCagg and Mabel Boardman.

Ushering the parishioners to their seats would have been two senior trustees of the church, Justice John Marshall Harlan and Robert Shaw Minturn, older brother of the four beautiful sisters. Harlan would become one of the most courageous of United States Supreme Court Justices known for his dissent, championing civil rights, in the *Plessey v. Ferguson* decision which approved "separate but equal" facilities for whites and blacks. A Sunday school teacher in Washington, D.C., despite his demanding court schedule, Harlan was to have just one more year in Murray Bay, dying soon after he returned to Washington in October 1911. His grandson, John Marshall Harlan II, who spent summers in Murray Bay, also served on the U.S. Supreme Court.

A year before, Robert Minturn and his wife, Bertha Potter Minturn, had ordered a bell from Thomas & Company in Leicestershire, England to be installed in the tower after the church was clad in stone. After his death, friends would give an iron clock for the front of the church in memory of Justice Harlan. It had not worked for years, but spontaneously started one month before the 100th anniversary of his death.

The Organist began to play the first notes of the processional hymn "Holy, Holy, Holy." As the congregants sang the familiar words "...all the saints adore thee, casting down their golden crowns around the glassy sea..." many might have looked out the church windows on the sparkling, calm St. Lawrence.

CHAPTER TWO

The Minturns

"I will never forget the views over the hills and the cottages by the shore. I was delighted by the simple life, different than I had ever seen before, and the most wonderful sunsets..."

—Newton Phelps Stokes

Minturn family on the lawn
Murray Bay Protestant Church collection

Years later, Newton Phelps Stokes recalled sitting with Edith and friends by a bonfire at night, "listening to native songs and watching the habitants dance simple, awkward dances with great delight."

Seated in front of the Minturn daughters in the Murray Bay Protestant Church on that August day in 1910 was the formidable Susanna Shaw Minturn, who took pride in being the first American woman to purchase land in Murray Bay and build a house on the shore of the St. Lawrence. By that time, she had built two clapboard houses with wide verandas, decorating them with the white wooden furniture of local craftsman and woven tapis or rugs in bright local colors on the plank floors.

Her first house was designed by Beaux Arts architect, Charles McKim, a suitor of her daughter, May. The square house in the popular neo-colonial style and clad in cedar shingles and stone was completed just in time for Edith's wedding. For a few years, it and the church shared Murray Bay's most prominent point, one day to be shared by some of its most famous residents.

Robert Shaw Minturn
Murray Bay Protestant Church collection

McKim's partner, Stanford White, would later come to Murray Bay to design a villa down the beach from Susanna's house for Brooklyn's mayor and then Senator Alfred C. Chaplin, who knew that Stanford White was the grandest of Gilded Age architects. Ever notorious in his relationship with young Ziegfeld Follies chorus girls, White liked the salmon fishing close by. Chaplin's daughter would marry Hamilton Fish, whose family is thought to have been one of the most significant dynasties in the United States Congress, along with the Kennedys.

Susanna's son-in-law, Newton Phelps Stokes, had supplied the design for what was known as the "second Minturn House" on the other side of the church with a wide veranda overlooking the water, stretching away from the river and a long wing for servants. Still standing today, the house is little changed and a tribute to Susanna and Phelps Stokes. Unlike others of their set who filled their Newport mansions with heavy French furniture, English hunting scenes, and crystal chandeliers, the Murray Bay homes utilized the artisans of the area whose simplicity would be seen as chic and modern. Susanna Minturn's houses overlooked the rocky beach just below where she could observe her children and grandchildren, some very daring who plunged into the waters not warmer than 50 degrees, even in summer. At least twice during summer, the Minturns marveled at double rainbows, seemingly proof of Murray Bay magic. The rainbows stretched across the St. Lawrence River, fifteen miles wide at that point, seeming to begin at the village of Cap a l'Aigle on the north, Kamouraska on the south.

Although Susanna Shaw Minturn always dressed in black following the deaths of her little boy, Francis, at age six and her husband, Robert Bowne Shaw, eleven years later, hers was a life of action, not mourning. She stood erect and wore her pure white hair like a crown. Her early beauty was unmistakable. Everyone said she was a force to be reckoned with, famously using her open parasol to warn traffic as she crossed Fifth Avenue from her Gramercy Park home. Her own great beauty had been extolled in the 1860s by a Higginson, ancestor of legendary garden creator and possibly Charlevoix's most beloved resident, Francis Cabot. He confided to a relative that she was one of the most beautiful creatures he had ever seen.

Born in 1839, Susanna came from a family of Boston abolitionists, the most famous being her brother, Colonel Robert Gould Shaw, immortalized by the Gilded Age's most famous sculptor Augustus St. Gaudens. Colonel Shaw, a handsome young white man, is depicted astride a horse and appearing rigorously strong—buttons almost bursting from his coat. Shaw is the central figure in the monument to the first African-American troop to fight in the Union army. The monument stands across from the Massachusetts State House on the Boston Commons. His death in 1863 at the Battle of Fort Wagner was the subject of the 1989 movie, "Glory."

Robert Gould Shaw Memorial

Susanna's own mother, Sarah Blake Shaw, had been a lifelong friend of Elizabeth Barrett Browning and her husband, Robert. Sarah had encouraged her daughter to be an independent thinker. Her father, Francis George Shaw, was heir to a Boston shipping fortune, but turned his back on city life to live close to Brook Farm in Massachusetts, an intellectual and idealistic community visited by some of the great minds of the time. He also took the whole family to live in several European countries and their children learned a number of languages.

In his memoirs, Susanna's son-in-law, Newton Phelps Stokes, recalled visiting Sarah Shaw in Paris with his wife Edith, Sarah's granddaughter, soon after their marriage.

35

"She lived at 30 Rue St. Dominique and was always so happy to welcome you and hear the latest gossip. She was always conversed on current events and very forward thinking. She was dressed in widow's black, but her hair was covered with ribbons and lace and she always wore long white gloves."

Susanna and her daughters later marched in Albany for women's rights in 1914 and Susanna encouraged her daughters not only to participate in the suffrage movement, but also to work for the needs of working women. Like Eleanor Roosevelt and Mary Harriman, Edith worked in the Settlement houses of New York City, very hands-on efforts not usually done by women in society.

Years later, Susanna's son-in-law, Newton Phelps Stokes, would write about Susanna in his memoirs.

"I remember her 20 years after we first met, still tall, active, erect and beautiful, sitting in her Gramercy Park home knitting socks for soldiers in the great war."

Susanna had married Robert Browne Minturn, Jr. whose father was a partner in the shipping firm of Grinnell, Minturn & Co., owners of the *Flying Cloud* and other fast and famous ships. The *Flying Cloud* set the record that stood for many years on the New York to San Francisco route around Cape Horn to the California Gold Rush.

Known for his dashing good looks and ready charm, Robert Browne Minturn, Jr. had graduated from Columbia University and travelled to exotic lands before marrying Susanna in 1862.

Living first in New York, they bought her parents' house on Staten Island, a quite fashionable neighborhood in 1865. Five of their seven children were born there. They had lived on Staten Island for sixteen years when their six year-old son, Francis, contracted diphtheria on Christmas Day and died twelve days later.

Robert Browne Minturn, Jr. died eleven years later of a heart attack. Many thought that it was the panic of 1882 and subsequent loss of fortune that led to his death. His family had to move to his family's Gramercy Park home and Edith wore a dress she already owned for her debut.

Edith and Newton Phelps Stokes, both 28 years old and beyond the usual marriage age of the day, had a brief courtship played out on the banks of the St. Lawrence River. They had met briefly as children on Staten Island where both the Minturn and Stokes families raised their children before moving to Gramercy Park. They met again in December 1894 when he sailed back from Paris where he was studying architecture at the Ecole Des Beaux Arts. Newton spent the Holidays with his parents at Shadow Brook, the spacious and grand new Stokes estate that his father, Anson Stokes, had constructed in the Berkshires.

This Tudor mansion on 900 acres close to Lenox, Massachusetts, had cost $500,000 to build and was thought to be the second largest residence in the country when it was constructed in 1893. Frederick Law Olmsted, landscape architect and friend of other Murray Bay residents, designed the gardens. Anson Stokes was injured in a riding accident there in 1898. His leg was crushed and after it was amputated, he moved to a mansion in Darien, Connecticut. Shadow Brook was sold to Andrew Carnegie in 1917. In 1956, Shadow Brook was sold to a monastery.

It was at a New Year's Day house party in 1895 at Shadow Brook when Newton saw Edith again and danced with her once. Later, he invited her out for a sleigh ride and dressed in what he imagined to be "a very fetching costume" he reported in his autobiography. "I chose a flowing blue tam-o-shanter cap and a blue and white speckled waistcoat. (Edith later reported that it would have been perfect for scarecrows.)

Although Newton declared his interest in marrying her, Edith didn't respond to his request and it was a long sleigh ride home. He returned to Paris to pursue his studies, but his thoughts remained with Edith. Newton recalled in his memoirs, it was Bob Minturn who said, "My sister is a fierce little thing, stay right here and take her off in a blaze of glory." Her sister Gertrude wrote to Newton advising him to come at once, that possibly his plea would get a positive response.

That summer, Phelps Stokes pursued Edith to Murray Bay. At the time, Susanna and her daughters were renting the spacious *Maison Rouge*, owned by Edward Blake, and then his son, William Hume Blake, Canadian aristocracy and leading members of the Murray Bay Protestant Church. Maison Rouge was perhaps the most famous of the older villas in Murray Bay, containing eight bedrooms and some said named for the Blakes' liberal politics, not the color it was painted. From the wide porch on Maison Rouge, Susanna could observe progress on her home below, next to the church that would be completed in July 1895, just in time for the wedding.

On a rainy day, as Edith and Newton walked along the Quebec road that led down from Maison Rouge to the rocky beach, Newton's marriage proposal was accepted at last. Just before they reached the wide piazza of Maison Rouge, they made their plan to marry later that summer at the Murray Bay Protestant Church. Almost forty years later, Newton would remember how beautiful Edith looked in a red cloak and hood.

The simple Murray Bay life was something different for Newton who had moved to Madison and 37th Street with his mother in 1867. The neighborhood was known as Murray Hill. They continued to enjoy the house on Staten Island in the spring and autumn. It was surrounded by seven acres of lovely gardens and lawns, and a bowling alley provided much enjoyment for the children. His grandfather owned three houses in a block on 37th Street, each built in 1853. Phelps, Dodge and Co. constructed the home at 231 Madison on the east corner of 37th which still stands today as part of the Morgan Library. A Murray Hill address meant that you were part of the elite society of Gilded Age New York, as described in Edith Wharton novels.

Writing in his memoirs, Stokes described the house: "[I]t was really a stately mansion with a suite of three drawing rooms, many mirrors and statues, including those of grandfather and mother which are now in our house in Greenwich."

A favorite pastime in his youth was playing with his eldest sister Sadie in the attic where there were trunks filled with letters and stereopticon photographs. In later years, he wondered if a letter from General Lafayette might have been among the letters preserved in the trunk. The French hero of the American Revolution had stayed with Newton's grandfather in 1824, before launching one of his numerable tours of the country.

His childhood was filled with happy and often humorous memories. At age eight, the daughter of Samuel F.B. Morse, the famous painter and inventor of the telegraph, was seated on the rug, playing blocks with him and his siblings. Other memories involved Jocko, his mother's favorite monkey, a beloved pet who sat frequently on her shoulder.

"Jocko loved to sit on the mantle and strike matches," he recalled in his memoirs. "One day we returned from church to find the fire department in the drawing room, having arrived just before Jocko's fire had taken the whole house up in flames."

Perhaps his fondest childhood memory was an elaborate Christmas party planned by his mother for her children and their friends. "I was five years old and a grand pie was brought in and when the crust was removed, several pigeons flew out and perched around the tea room."

Newton recalled frequently playing euchre with his grandfather. "When one of the older gentlemen who were his regular partners didn't appear for a scheduled game, I would be called upon to take his place. I played a fair game, but I was apt to get rattled and when I made a mistake the three old gentlemen glowered at me."

Judy Carmack Bross

As the New York *Sun* reported, "Miss Minturn's beauty has given her more than a local name. Her poses in tableaux vivants for charitable objects have attracted the attention of artists. Most recently, she posed for the Statue of the Republic in the Court of Honor at the World's Columbian Exposition. A photograph of the pose won for the photographer first prize in the last exposition of the society of photographers."

Edith Minturn Stokes: The Golden Lady
World's Columbian exposition collection

It was thought that Daniel Chester French had observed Edith in a tableau vivant at a party and knew that she would be the model for the statue who proudly holds a scepter and staff above her flowing gown. The tableau vivant, often performed at parties at home as described in Edith Wharton's House of Mirth, featured society beauties bringing alive works of art or history by posing behind gauzy curtains dressed in costumes to reveal their characters. Edith was thought to be one of the most skilled as well as the most beautiful.

Details of Edith's and Newton's wedding were revealed in the society pages of the times, including guests who travelled from Lenox and Bar Harbor for the August 21st wedding. Edith's going away attire was detailed in a fashion magazine of the day which noted that she had selected "[a] dull green dress dotted with warm reds for crossing the continent." Her taste, they revealed was very fashion forward—Edith would set a trend for more fitted sleeves, eschewing puffy or leg o' mutton sleeves of the high Victorian era and foreshadowing her modern mode portrayed by John Singer Sargent where she stands looking directly at the viewer, straw boater in hand, looking as if she had just walked off the Stokes' tennis court on Staten Island.

That Edith and Newton were members of the highest social echelon was obvious to all, even though they chose a tiny church on the St. Lawrence River for their wedding.

Three years later, both are mentioned prominently in a New York *Times* column, "What's Going on in Society" of October 25, 1898, in a wedding that could not have been more different than the one chosen by the Stokes, for whom the beauty and simplicity of a Murray Bay wedding was what they wanted.

"The wedding of Harold Herman Baring and Miss Marie Churchill at the fashionable St. James Church brought the largest group of curious spectators since the wedding there of the Duke and Duchess of Marlborough. Although an attempt had been made to prevent a crowd in the church by the issuance of cards of admission, hundreds of women obtained entrance on one pretext or another. It was impossible to keep a passage open for guests. During the ceremony, women climbed over the backs of pews and stood on footstools on the seats to get a better look."

Newton and Edith's brother, Robert Shaw Minturn, were among the groomsmen reported to have been wearing "diamond safety pins which glittered on their white ascot scarves, while Edith was described as exquisite in shrimp pink satin with a black hat.

Phelps Stokes' autobiography, *Random Reflections of a Happy Life,* is filled with both humility and humor about their early years as a married couple.

"I remember Mr. Sargent as a delightful companion and we shall never forget the pleasant mornings in his attractive studios. Mr. Sargent wanted to have Edith pose with a Great Dane, but when she was ready to pose he discovered that his friend who owned the dog had left town and taken his Great Danes with him. He painted me in the painting in three standings, really I was an accessory."

That painting had been a wedding present for the young couple from James A. Scrimser. When Edith died in 1937 at age 70, the painting was given as a bequest to the Metropolitan Museum of Art where it now resides in Salon 771. Even though it is huge in size, measuring 84.25 inches by 39.75 inches, the Stokes had hung it in several of their residences following a cross-country tour of the painting as was the custom of the day. Today, it hangs today in a gallery devoted to Sargent paintings across from a portrait of Newton's parents, Anson and Helen Louisa, painted in a similar informal manner a year later in 1898.

Mr. and Mrs. Isaac Newton Phelps
Metropolitan Museum of Art collection, New York.

Although that is the iconic image of Edith, her grandson Newton P.S. Merrill said that Cecilia Beaux's portrait of Edith is the one his grandfather most loved.

Edith Minton Stokes
Portrait by Cecilia Beaux
From a Private Collection

Before Newton renewed his acquaintance with Edith, he had lived a life adventurous for a New York aristocrat, marked by the love of travel, knowledge and beautiful things. The World's Columbian Exposition of 1893 was something that Edith and Newton had in common, although they didn't know it at the time.

While Edith had posed for Daniel Chester French's statue of the republic, Newton had travelled through exotic destinations in the Far East with A.B. de Guerville, Special Emissary of the World's Fair to foreign courts. De Guerville had met with Bertha Palmer, the chair of the Women's Delegation and one of the most important creators of the Fair, and other leaders, and was charged to get the support of world leaders for the Chicago effort. The work would be labeled a success for many of the forty-six countries visited would set up displays at the Fair to the marvel of over 27 million visitors during the six months it was open.

The young man's own passion for the exotic led him to try to purchase a striking gift for the Metropolitan Museum in New York. "Sailing up the Irrawaddy River on my way from Rangoon to Mandalay, I spied a 10-foot, one-eyed idol which I bought as a gift for the Met. Unfortunately, it never arrived."

It is a testament to the endearing and enduring love of Edith that another treasure he spotted in his travels did find its way back to America.

"When I had travelled to Florence several years earlier, I was very taken by a mantelpiece which I reluctantly didn't buy. When Edith and I visited Florence on our honeymoon, Edith discovered that the mantle had been broken up into entablatures. She refused a pearl pin that I wanted to give her and said we should spend our money on the entablature instead. It has always stood on the mantle in our library in whatever location we lived since then."

Newt Merrill describes his grandfather as "an early Bohemian." "While studying at the Ecole des Beaux Arts and drifting around the world, he collected a wealth of stuff, prints and all sorts of things. Throughout his life he brought wonderful artistic friends home to meet his family."

Childless for many years, Newton and Edith adopted a four-year old girl on a visit to England whom they named Helen, for his mother. On the sunny day when the church celebrated the culmination of Newton's plans which encased the church in stone, six-year-old Helen cuddled between her parents at the first pew of the church and their devotion to her always shone on their faces.

"My mother worshipped her father and spent many years being his point person," Newt Merrill said. "She thought he was just the best and I believe she was not as close to her mother. I was probably all of five years old when he died, but I remember his taking a train out to Bedford where we lived for Sunday lunch and then rushing back to the city. New York was always the center of the universe to him."

Newton Stokes would devote much of his life to painstakingly researching and writing his six-volume "Iconography of Manhattan Island," his tribute to the city, from Dutch village to magnificent metropolis, required exhaustive research on almost each block of the city and depleted his energy and finances. Bad real estate investments had contributed as well to his decline in fortune. Edith stood by his side, supporting him with great love and devotion.

He served the city he wrote about with such passion in other ways. Like Edith, he was deeply committed to social reform. He was co-author of the Tenement House Law of 1901, with Edith's encouragement. During Franklin Delano Roosevelt's presidency, Newton served as head of the New York Art Commission and oversaw WPA murals at LaGuardia Airport, Harlem Hospital, and the New York Public Library.

"They lived such a different life then, but my grandparents were very dedicated to improving housing conditions, insuring proper plumbing and heat for the settlement houses," Newt Merrill said.

His architectural works stand today as testaments to his abilities. St. Paul's Chapel at Columbia University and the union settlement house are built with both beauty and functionality in mind. The second Minturn house, designed in an L-shape, perhaps with a memory of the much grander Shadow Brook in the Berkshires, functions today with the same versatility for family and guests as it did almost 120 years ago. The simple elegance of the Murray Bay Protestant Church clad in stone is perhaps the most beloved structure from Gilded Age Murray Bay that exists today.

"Most of his buildings have been torn down but he was a fine architect who came in second in the design competition for many major structures," Newt Merrill said. "I always loved the Sherman Hoyt House in New York which stood on the northwest corner of Park Avenue and 79th Street which my grandfather built in 1917.

Constructed in fieldstone in a Tudor style, it was torn down in 1971. In 2012, New York *Times* critic Christopher Gray wrote about his sadness in seeing the building about to be bulldozed. "If it had been enlarged 40 times it could have been a rival for Downton Abbey. It seemed so permanent, what millionaire would not have wanted to have lived there?"

As a child, Newt Merrill visited his grandparents' home in Greenwich, Connecticut where the Sargent painting hung for many years. "It was an extraordinary place. Every piece came from a castle in England, with each piece numbered so it could be reassembled to appear that it had stood there for centuries. The house sat up on Round Hill and could be seen for a distance."

51

Judy Carmack Bross

With his unfailing generosity and gratitude to
the community that played such an important part
in Edith's life, Newton took delight in working up
the drawings which were used to clad the Murray
Bay Protestant Church in stone. The little church
would always remain strong in his memory. The
communal aspects of religion, as well as the power
of prayer always played a part in his life. "I
remember watching my parents kneeling in prayer
at night," he wrote. "They were so still and quiet
for such a long time that I thought that they might
be asleep."

More than twenty years after the August 20,
1910 celebration at the Murray Bay Church, he
wrote:

"Were I asked what single principle or habit on
my part has brought me the greatest satisfaction,
rather not an elaborate set form, but simple
communion with God. I am an optimist when I
think of God's wisdom and love."

Throughout their lives together, Edith and
Newton never lost their love for each other or their
joint love for beauty and adventure. Although the
exact reason for Edith's physical decline is
unknown, it was thought to be a type of
hypertension that today could be cured by a variety
of treatments. In her sixties, Edith suffered a series
of strokes that left her almost paralyzed. Newton
rarely left her side, reading novels and histories to

her. Edith died in 1937 at age 70. Newton died in 1944. He begins his memoirs:

"Mrs. Stokes did like the way certain events were treated." Every reference to his wife was a testament to the enduring strength of their marriage.

"My grandfather had managed to lose his funds in the Crash. He downsized and had in a small apartment in New York, living a modest life until his death in 1944," Newt said.

Robert Shaw Minturn and his wife, Bertha Potter, called "Lillie" by family and close friends, occupied the pew with his mother that August day in 1910. The Minturns were major church supporters from the earliest days. Robert served as Trustee from 1900 until 1913 and as Treasurer for three years. A Harvard graduate and lawyer, Robert Minturn was a close friend of Edith Wharton and Henry James. He and Lillie married in 1906, but they never had children. Right out of Harvard, Bob Minturn accepted a job with J.P. Morgan and worked on Wall Street for many years. Minturn led the church in making what was perhaps its most important decision—to clad the wooden church in the native stone of the area, thus preserving it from the fires that destroyed almost all the other churches in the town at some point and many of the magnificent clapboard villas.

Bob Minturn and Newton Stokes had been friends dating from their early days on Staten Island. In his memoirs, Newton recalled: "In 1892, I had the opportunity to buy one of the first 50 bicycles in America and Bob Minturn got one of the first as well. We learned together on long paths on the Stokes' seven-acre Staten island estate."

Hugh Minturn, the youngest of Susanna Shaw Minturn's children, would not be present that celebratory late summer day. On June 25, 1910, he married Ruth Windsor and was on his honeymoon. Also absent was the youngest of the four beautiful Minturn sisters, Mildred Minturn Scott.

Even as a young girl, Gertrude Minturn Pinchot's beautiful daughter, Rosamond, was in the blinding eye of 1920s paparazzi because of the exotic way she lived out her short fame, displaying a rashness seen later in her cousin, Edie Sedgwick, whose father, Francis, felt that she would turn out like Rosamond. Helen Stokes Merrill, daughter of Edith and Newton Phelps Stokes, remembered that during an argument at lunch with her brother, Gifford, Rosamond picked up a knife and headed toward him.

Rosamond Pinchot with her mother and son

Rosamond was just nineteen in October 1923 when she and her mother Gertrude boarded the *RMS Aquitania*, known as the "Queen of the Cunard Line" in Cherbourg, France. Mother and daughter had delighted in a Parisian shopping spree and were returning to New York with trunks full of formal attire for her debut on December 20th.

Gertrude and her millionaire husband, Amos

Pinchot, had divorced when Rosamond was thirteen. Pinchot was a wealthy lawyer and a key figure in the Progressive Party who helped fund the socialist magazine, "The Masses." Almost six feet in height and glorious in looks, Rosamond caught the eye of theater impresario, Max Reinhardt, as she boarded the ship. He saw instantly that she was the beauty he wanted to star in his Broadway play, "The Miracle" to be done in pantomime.

Often described as "spectacles," Reinhardt's plays were nothing if not symbolic, filled with the influence of Wagner and German Expressionism. Reinhardt was born in Baden Bei Wien, Austria-Hungry. He was fifty when he spied the young woman whom he would later describe as "part animal, part Grecian goddess" as she boarded the luxury liner. After many auditions in both Europe and America, he had found no one to play the part of the nun—and he wanted to cast Rosamond on the spot after observing the graceful, athletic teenager on the dance floor the first night out at sea.

The next morning, Reinhardt made his pitch to both Rosamond and her mother, undaunted that the spirited young girl had no acting experience. The role of the medieval nun Meglidis would be performed in pantomime. Even an adventurous young woman like Rosamond would have been captivated as she heard Reinhardt describe the play's staging.

Meglidis is lured by an evil piper from her cloister. The plot demanded that the nun run from place to place on a seven-year journey. This journey was transformed into a three-act play where there would be no audience as such. Instead, the ticket holders were required to serve as acolytes and cast members were jugglers, animals, merchants, and others who would wander among the ticketholders.

The glamorous aristocrat, Lady Diana Manners, daughter of the Earl of Rutland and later the wife of Duff Cooper, the Viscount Norwich, played the Madonna. The star's role involved much running around, perfect for an athlete like Rosamond.

"It came over me what a great chance I was missing. I realized that at last something I really wanted was being offered to me. I wanted the part of the nun more than anything I had ever wanted before, so I went to find Professor Reinhardt and tell him I was ready to act. Even though he did not speak English, I begged him to give it to me."

When the *Aquitania* docked in New York, gone were the plans for an excursion to Labrador and a possible trip with her father and brother to Hawaii after her debut so that she could learn to surf. Rosamond had her parents' reluctant agreement—it was hard to say no to the vibrant and determined Rosamond.

"The Miracle" was perhaps the high point of Rosamond's short life. Fourteen years later, she would commit suicide, when she was only 33. Helen Stokes Merrill recalled in *Edie: An American Biography* by Jean Stein.

"The part was nothing, no acting involved at all. Rosamond was just required to run (I think she was escaping the convent) up one aisle of the theater, around the back and down another, in her habit and with her hair flying. Everyone was just fascinated. The play was a tremendous success. It ran about 300 performances or so on Broadway— and all of it went to Rosamond's head. She went into something else and was a total flop, and couldn't act at all. Years later, she committed suicide. She asphyxiated herself in the front seat of her car in the closed garage on a rented estate."

Like Edie Sedgwick, her decline was understandable, but she had much more than what Andy Warhol referred to as "15 minutes of fame."

The press called Rosamond "an actress of destiny," extolling the fact that she had given up her debutante year for the theater. One headline proclaimed, "Rosamond Pinchot passes some actresses who have spent lives on stage."

She often showed humor when describing her future, telling a reporter: "Well, I dream of entering the drama seriously, to star, and I am studying faithfully to that end, but I fear that perhaps after all this glory I may find myself announcing humbly next season, 'Madame, dinner is now served.'"

Following the Broadway run, Rosamond joined the cast for a United States tour and then accepted an invitation from Reinhardt to perform in "The Miracle" and "Midsummer Night's Dream" at the Salzburg, Austria festival. During a golden summer staying at Reinhardt's castle near the Alps, Rosamond received a gold-embossed plaque from the Austrian government thanking her for her performance as the nun.

Returning to New York to once again play the nun, Rosamond turned twenty-one and papers praised the fact that the rich girl is happy because her father lets her work. Both Amos and Gertrude encouraged their young daughter to work, something unusual for a young girl in 1923, particularly one so wealthy. She lived with her mother at the corner of 81st Street and Fifth Avenue, an easy walk to Central Park where she rode her horse, a French hunter named Fleury.

Her circle of friends included Clare Booth Brokhaw (later Clare Booth Luce), George Cukor, and the Douglas Fairbanks, and Zoe Atkins. While waiting for other parts, she hosted parties, wrote in her diary, took acting and ballet lessons, and attended intimate dinners at the home of publisher Conde Nast, and the William Randolph Hearsts. At the Beaux Arts Ball at the Astor Hotel, she met the tall athletic war hero, "Big Bill" Gaston. Like Rosamond, he came from a distinguished Boston family and his grandfather had been governor of Massachusetts.

While dating Big Bill, Rosamond was cast by the highly regarded film director George Cukor, famous for *Adam's Rib*, *Little Women*, and *The Philadelphia Story* to name a few of his never-to-be-forgotten films. Rosamond's film, "Pardon My Glove" would not belong amongst those movies, although her co-star, Billie Burke, (Glinda, the good witch in *The Wizard of Oz*) was never to be forgotten.

Of the fascinating Rosamond, the press wrote:

"Her favorite color is red. Her apartment, a penthouse in the East Seventies features large red flowers in white vases against white walls. She plays backgammon, but never bridge. Her favorite drink is a Haitian rum cocktail. She smokes a lot in public, but never alone."

But like her cousin Edie Sedgwick, Rosamond's "celebrity-hood" passed quickly and she was left with demons intent on destroying her. Mental instability, depression, and tragedy had marked the family and would continue to do so.

Rosamond's half-sister, Mary Pinchot Meyer, would die in an unsolved murder in 1964 at the age of 44. A beautiful socialite and painter, Meyer was believed to have had trysts with President Kennedy at the White House and she was rumored to have brought along marijuana and LSD to most of these meetings. She'd first met the future president at a dance at Choate Rosemary Hall in 1938. She later left Vassar to become a journalist, working for United Press and *Mademoiselle*. She had married Cord Meyer who was appointed a principal operative of the CIA by Allen Dulles and it was rumored that she also had worked for the CIA. In 1983, LSD guru and Harvard lecturer, Timothy Leary, claimed that she contacted him in 1962 to tell him of her plan to avert worldwide nuclear war by convincing powerful male members of the Washington establishment to take mind-altering drugs that would cause them to ignore the Cold War. Her murder on a walking path in Georgetown remains unsolved, with rumors that she feared for her life after the Kennedy assassination forever surrounding the mystery. Meyer's biographer, Nina Burleigh, wrote: "She wore manners and charm like a second skin."

In the last years of Rosamond's life, she worked with Thornton Wilder on his first production of "Our Town," ending her life between the opening nights of the play in Boston and

Philadelphia. The *Philadelphia Ledger* would write: "[t]he plot of the new play in which death is depicted as more beautiful than life may have inspired Rosamond Pinchot to commit suicide."

In August 1910, Rosamond was just a little girl happy to fidget with her cousins in church and then romp out for a glorious summer's day of play. Many of her later summers would be spent in her father's magnificent mansion called "Grey Towers" in Milford, Pennsylvania and she would miss the opportunity to be influenced by Edith and Newton Phelps Stokes. More than any other family members, theirs was the life to revere for the love and respect they showed one another while serving others on a large scale.

Perhaps on August 10, 1910 Rosamond looked up at her beautiful aunt and caught for a moment the strength and purpose that was there. But the sermon was beginning and little Rosamond and her cousins were shushed by her mother, Gertrude.

Edith and Newton would have hoped that the preacher for the 1910 celebration would have been the Reverend William Rainsford, former Rector of St. George's Episcopal Church in New York, who spent extended summers in Murray Bay, often renting his own cottage. Because it is a summer church, no permanent clergy are appointed, but prominent ministers from both the United States and Canada would delight in spending a few weeks each summer in the paradise that is Murray Bay. Parishioners housed the visiting ministers in their elaborate Boulevard homes. Visiting the sick and fundraising for a building fund were not part of their duties.

Dr. Rainsford was a crusading reformer, immersed in labor causes. He encouraged Edith and Newton in their Settlement House efforts. He eliminated the common practice of families paying for the rental of church pews in his own church. An extremely handsome man with passionate beliefs, he attracted many women followers. It is said that on an ocean liner carrying Reverend Rainsford and his good friend, J.P. Morgan, to Europe, a young woman chose Rainsford over the multi-millionaire.

By 1910, Dr. Rainsford had suffered a physical collapse due to his tireless reform efforts and could not be in Murray Bay for the celebration of the renovation work Newton had headed, but perhaps Edith and Newton would be remembering when he had performed the marriage ceremony for them there on almost the same date in August, fifteen years before.

Dr. Rainsford had written: "I have known one or two women as beautiful as Edith, one or two as spiritual, but as for the combination, I have never known her equal."

CHAPTER THREE

The Tafts

Once there was a President
whose name was William Taft,
He came to La Malbaie
on a great big river raft.
And when he saw the Pointe-au-Pic
He said, "that's one for me!"
I'll go ashore and build a house
and raise a family."

From a Taft family song sung at many
joyful Murray Bay occasions.

Because he believed that a sitting President should
not have a summer White House outside the
United States, President Taft and his wife rented a
summer cottage in Beverly, Massachusetts in the
summer of 1910. The Tafts missed Murray Bay in
the summer, having rented or owned there since
1892, but even when he was not there, his jovial,
genial personality hovered in the air. It was not
only that United States Supreme Court justices
Taft and John Marshall, who received a relatively
low salary, could spend their long summer

vacations in a beautiful area with a fine home and a large local staff, but they could truly get away from all the pressures of politics.

William Howard Taft lured many people to Murray Bay by the force of his encouraging personality and the amicable leadership which attracted friends all his life. Perhaps he would tell friends, as he wrote to Theodore Roosevelt from Murray Bay in July of 1906, "I feel a boyish feeling—I'd like to jump up and down and shout."

Taft family on porch in Murray Bay
Musée de Charlevoix collection

A reporter once noted "his capacity for personal intimacy" and he was praised during his presidential campaign for his "good nature, indifference to self, apparently infinite patience and the ability to get along with men however cold and acerbic or crotchety they might be."

The future President had grown up in Cincinnati, Ohio, and when his boyhood home was placed on the National Survey of Historic Sites and Buildings by the National Park Service, S. Sydney Bradfort, the Historic Sites Historian, wrote this in the nomination of the site:

"America has produced few men who have led such a varied and successful life as William Howard Taft. Who else has been the Solicitor General of the United States, a federal judge, an eminently successful proconsul in the American empire, a vigorous secretary of war, a good President and an excellent chief justice of the supreme court...and a Yale man?"

The 37th President of the United States, serving from 1909 until 1913, William Howard Taft would perhaps have followed a strictly judiciary path to the Supreme Court if it hadn't been for his intelligent and encouraging wife, Nellie. As a teenager she had visited the White House as a guest of President and Mrs. Rutherford B. Hayes, who were family friends in Cincinnati.

Thirty years later, when Taft was made a member of Theodore Roosevelt's cabinet, she said that "the allure of the White House has never dimmed." In an interview with a journalist, Nellie recalled every detail. "Nothing in my life realizes the climax of human bliss which I felt as a girl of 16 when I was entertained at the White House."

Soon after that party, she confided to "Uncle Rutherford" that she "intended to marry a man who would be president." Hayes replied, "I hope you may, and be sure you marry an Ohio man."

That she did, and she made sure that Taft's political ascent kept him in the presidential trajectory. Although her parents wished debutante days and an early marriage for their daughter, Nellie taught at a boy's school in Cincinnati, worked for the beginning of the kindergarten system, not previously part of traditional education, and read constantly. Although Nellie turned down Taft's first proposal of marriage in 1885, she soon changed her mind.

"You will be my companion, my love, my life. I love you for your noble and consistent character," Taft wrote.

She remained constantly ambitious for him, listening to his speeches, every week entertaining large groups of government officials and their wives in Washington, D.C. when he served as Secretary of War, and worked side by side with him on his career. She became a liberated woman in some ways, being among the first to wear a short skirt, smoke, and espouse causes such as abating infant mortality. A lifelong lover of music, even though her parents would not agree to fund piano lessons, Nellie founded the Cincinnati symphony orchestra.

When she became First Lady, she was soon regarded by many as the finest woman in that demanding role. On the day of her husband's inauguration, Nellie chose to do what no other first lady before her had ever done—accompany her husband in the carriage which drove them from the Capitol to the White House.

Loving the White House gardens, she moved official occasions outdoors. Invitations went out to over 500 people for Friday afternoon garden parties when the Marine Band played. Men wore white coats and straw hats and women wore white dresses and carried colorful parasols. Creating the Potomac Basin and bringing the first Japanese cherry trees to the capitol were among her accomplishments.

Sadly, her effectiveness lessened when she suffered a stroke in 1909 soon after her husband became President. Partially paralyzed on her left side, Nellie was unable to speak. Through the constant efforts of herself and her family, she learned to say greetings and insisted on welcoming guests, but often she could not control her words and they could be inappropriate. Soon after the stroke, the Tafts made Beverly, Massachusetts their summer home, but both were delighted to return to Murray Bay after Taft's loss to Woodrow Wilson in 1913. When the President served as Secretary of War, Mrs. Taft had often taken their three children, Helen, Robert, and Charley, the youngest, to Murray Bay. She summered there in the years following her husband's death. Later in her life she recovered her speech and outlived her husband by thirteen years.

Charley Taft's son Peter still summers in Murray Bay in a house built on Taft Hill on the exact location of the beloved and rambling Taft house which burned down. Peter recalls his father and others saying that Nellie was a very strong woman who always spoke her mind.

A family history written by Helen Taft Manning, the only daughter of the President and a Professor of History at Bryn Mawr College, relates with energy how this Cincinnati family put Murray Bay first in their hearts. Helen Taft was married at the Murray Bay Protestant Church and continued to summer there with many members of the extended Taft family until her death in 1987.

Judy Carmack Bross

Helen Taft Manning
Musée de Charlevoix collection

Today, in addition to Peter and his wife, Diana Todd, there are several Tafts who make Murray Bay their summer home. Former Ohio Governor Bob Taft and his wife, Hope, live in a classic Charles Warren Home. Like President Taft, Bob is known for his friendliness and a fine golf game.

Helen Taft Manning wrote that 1892 was a remarkable year in the history of Cincinnati as well as of Murray Bay. Horace Taft, Taft's youngest brother, was to marry Winifred Scott of Niagara Falls and William Howard Taft and his family were among the many Cincinnatians who attended the wedding at Niagara Falls. A wedding guest who

70

had previously visited William Hume Blake, whom Helen Manning refers to as "the unquestioned ruler of the English-speaking colony in Murray Bay in 1892," encouraged them to push on to Murray Bay rather than return to Cincinnati.

The slogan for the Richelieu and Ontario steamboats at that time was "from Niagara to the sea" and that became the slogan of the Taft party as well. They boarded the Saguenay steamboat in Montreal, which made almost fifteen stops before dropping them off at the dock in the Pointe-au-pic entry to the heart of Murray Bay. Their first sight would have been Micmac Indians selling woven willow baskets beside a high cliff.

President Taft had written to Madame Chamard, proprietaire of Chamard's Lorne house, that there would be twenty-two in their party, including Helen Manning, the youngest explorer at the age of nine months. Named for the Marquis of Lorne, who was Governor General of Canada and had married a daughter of Queen Victoria, the house was perched on a bluff overlooking the port and what would become Taft Hill in the decades ahead.

The Taft children soon changed its name to "Forlorn House" due to its lack of electricity, running water and toilets, but they quickly learned to make do with oil lamps and wood stoves, and took to the outdoors with gusto. The Tafts stayed at

Chamard's for the summer. Many other distinguished summer travelers would board at Chamard's. It would one day become the Manoir Richelieu Hotel, famous today for one of the most breathtaking golf courses and green copper spired buildings.

During their second summer, the Tafts rented a cottage just down the road from Lorne House. Afterwards they moved to a summer rental on Taft Hill named Fassifern Cottage, built some twenty years before the Tafts arrived, which possessed not only a spectacular view, but secret caves for exploring, ponds to canoe, and woods for secret playgrounds.

For William Howard Taft, golf was a lifelong love and he would later say that he enjoyed being president of the Murray Bay Golf Club more than being president of the United States. The golf club was established in 1876, the fourth golf club built in Canada, and was located close enough for Taft's daily pleasure.

Young golf caddies, Murray Bay Golf Club
Musée de Charlevoix collection

In 1896, Taft decided that more room was needed for a course and he and a group of other enthusiastic golfers rented fields stretching out from where the Murray Bay Golf Club house stands today. This lease was based on the condition that cows should be pastured on the

73

links at night and on Sundays. The plus of this arrangement was that the cows acted as lawnmowers for the green, the minus is obvious. Soon a rule was made that the golfer could move his ball should it have landed in an unpleasant place. Taft would have been responsible for raising funds to buy the land and expand it around 1925.

Like Lorne House, Fassifern had no electricity, bathrooms, or running water. Helen Manning wrote that the Tafts built the first bathroom in Murray Bay and remembered that friends would come to take baths in it, often after they had finished a round of golf with Taft.

Building was inexpensive in Murray Bay and Charles Warren quickly added fireplaces and more bedrooms for the growing family. Finally, the house was re-built and had twenty bedrooms and twelve baths to accommodate all the children and grandchildren. Soon it became a compound, with extra cottages for more babies and their nurses.

At Taft family parties, often held on the anniversary of President Taft's birthday, Helen Manning Taft recalled family lore with great enthusiasm.

"The telegraph office was in one of the little cottages at the bottom of our hill and the presiding genius was Madame Rousseau. She had a little employee who ran the errands, but who went home to supper at 5:30. At 6:00 exactly, there arrived a telegram for William Howard Taft, Secretary of War. It read as follows: "Revolution has broken out in Cuba. Come at once to Washington since I want you to go to Havana as soon as possible to settle terms of peace when war is over. (signed) Theodore Roosevelt."

Madame Rousseau may or may not have known who Theodore Roosevelt was, but she wasn't going to try to deliver a telegram after the little boy had gone home to supper. So my father missed the only boat and had to remain in Murray Bay for 24 hours. He did go to Cuba and settle that particular revolution under the Platt Amendment, but I can't tell you whether it would have been settled better if he had gotten there earlier."

An Historic Sites historian had written about the President's diplomatic abilities, noting his service as ambassador to the Philippines:

"Taft arrived in Manila in 1901 and left in 1903. His farewell left a void in the hearts of most Filipinos, for he had established the supremacy of civil rule and laid the basics of self-government. He had displayed a confidence in the islanders that others lacked, especially the military. Taft, with President McKinley's backing, had inaugurated an American policy that could only end in independence."

Equally important during their days in Manila was Nellie Taft who gave large garden parties that had complete racial equality. The Tafts would be criticized by other government and military representatives in Manila for this unheard of diversity, but Nellie in particular wouldn't have it any other way.

Malvina Harlan, wife of Supreme Court Justice John Marshall Harlan, wrote in her memoirs that many who knew the President in Murray Bay commented on his grace on the dance floor and his athletic ability. In the village of Pointe-au-pic, he was known affectionately as "le petit juge" and although he didn't speak much French, he was one of the most popular of the summer residents among the French Canadians.

Helen Taft Manning related to Taft's descendants:

"In those days there was homespun made from habitant wool which was dyed to any color you liked and everyone had to have a suit made which never fitted, but which was regarded as very beautiful nonetheless. There was a general movement to get a pair of homespun trousers made for my father and he was conducted down to the dressmaker, Madame Boulianne, who plied her trade on the village street. Madame Bouliannne, whom I remember as almost as large in the waist as my father, got down on her knees with a tape measure. It took her a long time to work her way around and every time she moved she would utter exclamations of wonder and admiration. The trousers came home, but I can't tell you how often my father wore them. But the final news which went around the village was that he had given them to his favorite tailor who had trousers made out of them for all of his six or seven little boys."

A later note on William Howard Taft appeared in the *New York Times* on October 25, 2013, under the headline "In struggle with Weight a Century ago, a diet from today." The article, with a handsome photo of the president in later years, seated on a wide piazza, almost definitely on Taft Hill, states that he struggled mightily to take weight off and was humiliated by cartoonists who delighted in drawing his corpulent figure. New research has found that his weight-loss program, including exercise and small portions of meats and vegetables, with no snacking, coincides with today's thinking although surgery and diet drugs were not options at that time. He employed a personal trainer known at the time as a "personal culture man."

Daily golf, fishing in the chilly streams, and hikes with his children and guests were musts in his Murray Bay routine. His diet of lean meat and local produce, along with this exercise regime allowed him to rightly boast in the summer of 1906 that he could get rid of an old scale and use one which only recorded up to 250 pounds.

He struggled all his life with his weight, having gained back all he had lost after he went to the White House in 1909, weighing 354 pounds when he left office. The rumor circulated that he had once become stuck in the White House bathtub. But he never gave up and when he died in 1930, he weighed only 280 pounds.

Bob, he was a senator
and Charley quite a boy.

Helen was the only girl,
her papa's pride and joy.

And these had thirteen children
who have mostly made their mark;

They are as diversified as
animals in the ark.

Taft family song. verse two

Members of the Taft family have served in leadership positions in Ohio, Massachusetts, and Rhode Island, having furnished a governor of Rhode Island and Ohio, two United States Senators, two members of the U.S. House of Representatives, an Attorney General, two Secretaries of War, and a Secretary of Agriculture, as well as mayors and other local officials.

William Howard Taft, the only man to serve as both President and Chief Justice of the United States Supreme Court, was one of Murray Bay's most beloved residents.

Taft on the golf course
Musée de Charlevoix collection

Judy Carmack Bross

CHAPTER FOUR

The Blakes and the Wrongs:
Canada's Aristocrats

"What are fifty years of Europe
to a summer at Malbaie?"
—William Hume Blake

William Hume Blake was a member of Murray Bay's most aristocratic Canadian family which intermarried with the Wrong and Cronyn families. The elegant and talented actor Hume Cronyn was a member of the family and visited Murray Bay several times during his life with his wife, actress Jessica Tandy. Hume Cronyn's great-grandfather was the first Anglican bishop of Huron, which would become western Ontario, and his father, Hume Blake Cronyn, was a businessman and prominent member of parliament.

Helen Taft Manning, daughter of a U.S. President and member of an American Murray Bay dynasty, called William Hume Blake "the unquestioned ruler of the English-speaking colony in Murray Bay."

William's father Samuel and his uncle, Edward Blake, had worked for the unification of Canada in 1867, the same year that the Murray Bay Protestant Church was built.

Samuel Hume Blake
Portrait by Notman of Montreal
Musée de Charlevoix collection

Samuel was the first Chancellor of Upper Canada. Both Samuel and his brother Edward were leaders in the early and precarious years of the new Canadian Federation. Samuel was an active layman in the church of Canada. He wrote many pamphlets on religious questions and was a founder of Wycliffe College in Toronto.

Edward, described by Henry Dwight Sedgwick as handsome, tall, and dignified, later left his position as head of the Liberal Party and accepted a seat in the British parliament to represent an Irish borough.

Edward Blake
Musée de Charlevoix collection

"These two eminent personages, and their families, gathered a group of young men around them, active, athletic fellows, fond of camping and fishing and golf, all bristling with an abhorrence of bringing citified ways into Murray Bay life," wrote Henry Dwight Sedgwick.

William Hume Blake
Private collection of Tommy Hoopes

On Sunday, August 20, 1910, Samuel and his son William would have been seated together in the sun-filled church with William's wife, Alice Jean Law. Samuel would live another four years.

In his book, *Memoirs of An Epicurean*, Henry Dwight Sedgwick described Samuel's Sunday School classes. "Mr. Sam Blake was a man of strong character and of very definite religious ideas. My wife, as a girl, used to attend his class in Sunday School and one Sunday when a British man-of-war dropped anchor off the wharf, the whole town rushed down to the wharf to see it and greet the sailors that were given shore leave. Mr. Blake told his class that the Devil was waiting round the corner at the dock to catch the soul of any girl who went down on the Sabbath day to see the ship or the sailors."

Born in 1861, William Hume Blake was considered to be fishing's finest writer. The author of *Brown Waters*, his expeditions with local guides led him to explore what would become L*e Park National de Laurentides*, close to Murray Bay. He translated into English the definitive French Canadian novel, *Maria Chapdelaine*, which told of the customs, pleasures, and great hearts of the local people. He wrote *In a Fishing Country* about his beloved Charlevoix region. For forty years he roamed the Laurentians, fished the lakes and streams, tracked the caribou, and became close friends with the "habitants" as the local people were known. It was said that William helped found the Murray Bay Golf club because it would give the women of the community something to do after church so that he could go fishing.

The romance of this lawyer turned ultimate sportsman lives on in Quebec. In 2013, today's noted Charlevoix author Jean des Gagniers published *William Hume Blake in Charlevoix*, which combines sections from Blake's book and other essays, translated into French:

"William dedicated *Brown Waters* to "The companion who knows how to go light and fare hard, who is friendly with rain and finds no road too long."

In 1977, two years before her death, William's cousin, Ethel Blake Maraini, would recall:

"We used to love going to the trout camp, a lovely place called Gravel. It was a great honor to be asked. We were only asked because our cousin, Will Blake, would get us two days a year. We had to walk in for two miles. That is where I learned to fly fish. When you caught trout, the guide cooked them for you right there. It was a heavenly place."

Gravel continues until today as a private fishing camp, still an honor to be invited. People still walk in, although some opt for a bumpy van ride. The trout caught by guests are still cooked right away for supper. And it is still a heavenly place.

"The Trou"
Courtesy of Elisabeth Bacque

William was a hero to both the French Canadian habitants and to fishermen around the world. A Toronto obituary from February 1924 relates his death and the numbers of people who came to the Murray Bay Protestant Church to give their respects:

"The body of the late William Hume Blake, Canadian author and son of the late Hon. S.H.

Blake, K.C. of Toronto, was brought by a small party of friends and relatives to Quebec, where it was transferred to a special train and taken to Pointe-a-Pic for burial.

"By his special desire, the ground beside the beautiful little stone church was to be his last resting place. In that Church he had been married and amid the scenery of the North Shore and the forests of the Laurentians, the happiest days of his life had been spent. He loved every stream and lake among the hills and the people of the district were his dearest friends. He knew and sympathized with the outlook of the French Canadians as few outsiders did and he devoted himself to the task of revealing that outlook to them. By his peculiarly beautiful translation of Hermon's *Marie Chapdelaine* he has touched the hearts of English readers the world over and has opened their eyes to the beauty and piety of the life of the French Canadian peasant. On its arrival at Pointe-a-Pic, the body was drawn in a sleigh to the church where the coffin was carried by his old woodland friends and guides from St. Urbain. The service was taken by Canon Scott and the church was filled with people from the village, paying a respectful homage to the dead.

"At the conclusion of the service, the body was carried by the bearers to the grave on the riverside of the church. There, among some silent spruces in a grave lined with evergreens, the dead was laid and the last prayers said. It was a most beautiful and fitting resting place for one who has drawn his life's inspiration from the hill and water scenery of the Lower St. Lawrence.

"To those who were privileged to be present at the funeral, the event will always be a wonderful memory. The day was cloudless and the air was as clear as that of Switzerland. The view from the graveside was superb. Ice floes drifted slowly down the river on the ebbing tide and the snow-covered hills of Cap à l'Aigle stood out against the blue sky. It was a scene of peace and beauty, full of the unspotted holiness of nature, and a worthy shrine for a Canadian who worked and loved his native land."

Despite the bitter cold, one sees in a photograph of that day hundreds of people lined up outside the Murray Bay Protestant Church to pay their respects to Blake.

No one wrote better than Blake of the poignancy of parting at the end of the summer:

"The busiest of men, on setting an unwilling foot in New York, straightway begins marking off the tedious procession of days that must pass before his return—that holds some families faithful unto the fifth generation and reunites others from the ends of the earth."

Blake recollects one visitor talking about the closing of his house, personifying furniture which dreads the long and lonely winter so much that holds onto the owners. "They have gone away by twos and threes. Groups making pretense of gaiety have stood upon the steamer's deck answering song with song, cheer with cheer, and as the distance widened, signal by signal. Solitary ones have departed in the night—so silently that the empty chair at breakfast first tells of their absence. Close up the ranks! Shorten the table! The break up is here, summer is over.

"And so comes the day when the house that has known so many carefree hours must be deserted. For the last time your footstep sounds in the darkened place. The very door handles seem loth to leave your grasp; the chairs extend their arms for an uncouth goodbye. You shut and bar the door through which the breeze has wandered at will all the long summer days. The clang hurts like an unkindness done to a creature suffering mutely, helplessly, at your hands.

"For surely these familiar walls have in them some sentiency—else how could they look such melancholy farewells....

"In the white desolateness of winter will not imprisoned echoes of laughter and music come forth—the very ghosts of sounds? To what dirge-like measure do you tread, while the house, half hidden in the trees, watches reproachfully your departure?

"The mist thickens—how it blurs everything!"

His sentiments echo today among summer residents as they say, at the end of the summer, "L'Annee Prochaine" — until next year!

The houses W.H. Blake would have been imagining were known as Maison Rouge, Milles Roches, and Le Caprice, the three most famous of the Blake Villas. Maison Rouge was the house that Edith, in her red cloak and Newton Stokes had returned to with the news that they were to be wed.

Susanna had rented the house in 1895 before her own Charles McKim house was finished. Justice John Harlan and his beautiful wife, Malvina, had rented it as well. And what a house it was, almost like another character in our story, the first of the great Murray Bay villas.

Blake family on the steps of Milles Roches
Top row: Rebecca and Samuel Blake.
Elisabeth Bacque collection

The striped socks worn by many of the children were characteristic of the Murray Bay region.

Edward and Margaret Cronyn Blake
and their children, circa 1903-04
Courtesy of Elisabeth Bacque

Paddling the Murray River was a passion of the whole Blake family. In private family papers, Gerald Blake orders a canoe for his father Edward who is serving in London:

"I will buy the canoe which I understand is a sixteen-foot basswood painted canoe, one inch wider and deeper than your usual model, but upon ordinary lines. I think that the price mentioned was $25.00, to include a pair of paddles. Please ship the canoe addressed, "Hon. Edward Blake, Pointe-a-Pic, Quebec and direct the Express Company to hand it over to The Richelieu & Ontario Navigation Company."

Like William, George McKinnon Wrong was a patrician and a writer, who two years before he attended church with his family on August 20, 1910, had chronicled the history of Murray Bay in *A Canadian manor and its Seigneurs.* Born in Ontario in 1860, Wrong was ordained as an Anglican minister and attendance each Sunday at the Murray Bay Protestant Church was of upmost importance to him. In 1894, he had become Professor and head of the Department of History at the University of Toronto.

In *A Canadian Manor and its Seigneurs,* he focused first on the majesty of Murray Bay's earliest beginnings:

"Here is the oldest of old worlds, in which pigmy man is not even of yesterday, but only of today. This majestic river, the mountains clothed in perennial green, the blue and purple tints so delicate and transient as the light changes, have occupied this scene for thousands of centuries. No other part of our mother earth is more ancient. The Laurentian Mountains reared their heads, it may be, long before life appeared anywhere on this peopled earth. No fossil is found in all their huge mass. In some mighty eruption of fire their strata have been strangely twisted. Since then sea and river, frost and ice, have held high carnival."

In 1886, George Wrong married Sophia Hume Blake, daughter of Edward Blake, Premier of

Ontario from 1871 until 1872 and leader of the Liberal Party of Canada from 1880-1887. Edward Blake built Le Caprice in 1898 and Sophia and George spent summers in that magnificent villa patterned on the style of the ultimate early Murray Bay "summer cottage," Maison Rouge, as well as at Maison Rouge itself. George and Sophie inherited Le Caprice upon the death of Edward Blake in 1912. Like Maison Rouge, Le Caprice was destroyed by fire shortly after they inherited it. The Blake family continued to build summer homes higher on the boulevard. George and Sophia had four children: a daughter Margaret who became a missionary; a son Edward, an Oxford academic; a son Humphrey, a diplomat; and a son Harold Verschoyle, a poet killed in World War I on July 1, 1916 at the Battle of the Somme, the first day of the battle.

Blake cousins and friend reading the news about the WWI
Courtesy of Elisabeth Bacque

A family photograph taken in August 1914 on a porch in Cap a l'Aigle, just across the bay from Murray Bay, shows a group of Blake cousins and friends reading the declaration of war in a local newspaper. Gerald Blake and Humphrey Hume Wrong enlisted in the British Expeditionary Force in June of 1915 because they had both studied at Oxford and felt that enlistment in the Canadian army wasn't happening fast enough. Harold Wrong had been the first to go to England to enlist, having been refused in Canada for medical reasons. Hume Wrong was the only cousin to survive the war. He studied at Oxford and became a professor of History at the University of Toronto before going on to a career in the foreign service. He would return to the cemetery in Pozieres British

Cemetery in Ovillers-La Boissele, France several times to visit the grave of his cousin Gerald. An uncle of Gerald, Colonel Robert Morris, married to his maternal aunt, served as an artillery officer with the British Army in Gallipoli and in Europe and was killed on March 25, 1917.

Harold and Gerald died at the battle of the Somme, in which during its first day alone almost 20,000 British troops were lost and 40,000 were wounded. Harold died on the first day, July 1, 1916. Gerald was killed on July 23, 1916, while leading his company on a night attack during the Battle of Pozieres Ridge. He was found where he had fallen, just short of the enemy trench, facing towards the enemy with a number of his men lying around him. Allied forces were attempting to break through German lines centered along a 25-mile front north and south of the river Somme. The battle lasted until November and in the end, 475,000 British and French soldiers had died. The Siege of the Somme has been used to demonstrate the futility of trench warfare. In the course of the battle, fifty-one Victoria crosses were won by British soldiers, including Harold Wrong.

Born in 1891, Harold was the second son of George Wrong and Sophia Blake. He graduated from University College in Toronto in 1913 with a degree in Classics and he began writing poetry before graduation. He played lawn tennis on his college team (a sport he perfected in Murray Bay), and received the McCaul medal for classics upon graduation. Soon after, he attended Christ Church College at Oxford on a Flavelle Travelling scholarship. He was back in Murray Bay in the summer of 1914 and immediately sought to join the first contingent of soldiers gathering at Valcartier, the Quebec training garrison, but was turned down for a health reason.

Determined to enlist, he returned to England to join the Oxford University Officers' Training Corps while studying at Oxford during the Michaelmas term. Soon afterwards, Harold was granted a commission as a second lieutenant with the 15th Lancashire Fusiliers. He joined his unit at Manchester and after ten months' training, chiefly in the north of England, went to France with that unit in November of 1915.

On June 30, 1916, Harold wrote a quick note to his older brother, Murray, who was living in England where he worked as Vice Principal of the Manchester School of Technology. Enclosed with the penciled note saying simply, "All well with me" was a pressed flower. His battalion was part of the 32nd division that held a sector in the southern part of the British line near Albert.

At 7:30 in the morning of July 1st, the battle of the Somme began. Among the 20,000 British troops was Harold Wrong, killed while leading his platoon against the German trenches. The last word heard from him came from a Private hit early in the advance. He reported that Lieutenant Wrong was wounded in the hand, but still led his men. His battalion was almost wiped out in the attack where machine gun fire thundered out of the ruined homes of Thiepval, a community on the Somme in Picardie. Of the 625 officers and men of his regiment who went over the top that morning, their objective being to take the village of Thiepval, some 470 men were killed, wounded, or declared missing.

Harold's body was never recovered. His name is inscribed on the Thiepval memorial along with those of 73,356 men who have no grave and are known to have fallen during the battle of the Somme.

Like many of the British poets, their works have been published posthumously. Two had been printed in *Chronicle of Wars* by English poets and others in *Arbor*, a magazine published at the University of Toronto, a publication Harold Wrong helped put together. In 1922, "Verses" by H.V. Wrong was published by his family. Previously unpublished poems had been found in loose sheets scattered among his papers.

On a summer's day in Murray Bay, Harold may have written the following poem, for it is known that he began composing poems at a young age:

Song

Oh! I could weave the beauty of the ocean,
Weave it in a web,
The Beauty of the Ocean,
And the tide's slow ebb.

And I could paint the glory of the mountains
Paint it in brilliant hue,
The glory of the mountains,
All their green and blue.

But who can tell the magic of your eyes,
Weave it or paint or sing,
The magic of your eyes
That knows no prisoning?

Harold wrote about death as he contemplated battle. This unpublished poem was found among his papers:

Death

I felt the clouds and all around me mist,
Behind, the twilight, a great flame before
That pierced the tick-spun texture of the clouds;
Behind it cleared, the mist was all in front.
I stood upon a pinnacle that rose
High in the air, and yet there was no height,
But all the world lay near within my grasp.
Light was my soul and my feet urged me on,
On through the grey that cloaked the distant flame;
I paused and looked, then forward turned once more
And forward strode into the foaming cloud,
And as I went the flame grew bright and wide,
And all was brilliant with that blazing light

Which dazzled me and filled my eyes with red
Till I was blinded and fell fainting down.
Then cleared the clouds and there was no more mist.

Harold's cousin, Gerald Blake, born on May 28, 1892 in Toronto, was the oldest son of Edward Francis and Ethel May Benson Blake. He had two younger sisters, Margaret and Constance, and a younger brother, Verschoyle Benson. Their father, a lawyer, had died in 1905 at the age of 39. His grandfather was the Hon. Edward Blake, PC, QC, who during his career was Premier of Ontario, a Member of Parliament, a Member of the British House of Commons and Chancellor of the University of Toronto. He studied at St. Andrews College and Bishop Ridley College, both in Ontario. He would spend the summer of 1910 in Murray Bay before entering University College at the University of Toronto with a double study in Classics and Mathematics that fall.

In 1914, he was admitted to the Law Society of Upper Canada and clerked with the law firm of Aylesworth, Wright, Moss & Thompson in Toronto and was a member of the Canadian Officer Training Corps at the University of Toronto. The night before he sailed to England, he asked Kathleen Ogden Jones to marry him. She followed him to England to complete her studies and always saved the letters her sweetheart wrote to her.

On the day before his death, Gerald wrote to his mother about the front:

"Of course, things are pretty sickening everywhere. There is not time to clear out all the trenches and open country of either the German or British dead. We people who are in it are the only ones who can realize for a moment what even a small advance means."

Hume Wrong, who was blind in one eye and was not accepted into the Canadian Army, had urged the cousins to enlist in England. It was he who wrote to Gerald's fiancée, Kathleen, that Gerald had died. Hume survived the war and after Gerald's death assisted Mrs. Blake in making arrangements for her son's gravesite in France. He sent home photographs from the cemetery that he visited in 1920. The area around the River Somme is a testament to the courage of men such as Gerald and Harold, with military cemeteries and many monuments commemorating the many from several countries who died on the battlefield.

On November 10, 2014 at Osgood Hall in Toronto, honorary admission to the Bar of the Law Society of Upper Canada was granted to sixty law students who did not survive the war, among them Gerald Blake. One of the representatives of the Blake family, Elisabeth Bacque, said: "...Members of all families were tracked down and invited and about 20 families were represented. We received a certificate and a book with the histories of all 60 men, an incredible work of research, and a very moving ceremony."

Ethel Constance Marani, Gerald's sister, was the photographer of the boys who read of the news of the outbreak of World War I on the porch at Cap a l'Aigle. She remembered that day 63 years later in a letter to her family.

"...the only way you could go to Tadoussac was by a little barge which they poled across the river. My brother and his cousin, Harold Wrong, went on a walking trip in 1914 and they camped on little lakes from Cap-a l'aigle and on towards Tadoussac. They saw a bear and had all sorts of adventures. When they came back to Cap-a-l'aigle, they heard the news that war had been declared. I have a lovely photograph that I took. They have the newspaper in front of them and oh the expressions on their faces, Carr Cronyn, Hume Wrong, my brother Gerald, and Harold Wrong. Carr had just had his appendix out. That is why he was down there with grandmother Blake. The boys had taken him on this trip rather reluctantly as they did not know whether he was well enough. He just left immediately and so did Harry Parker and Han Schlumberger (Boswell) and they all took the next boat away, as soon as they could."

Her own son, Major Peter Geoffrey Blake Marani, served as a Reserve Officer in the

Canadian Army with the Royal Regiment of Canada.

Not far from the front porch where the iconic family photograph was taken, there is a moving plaque on the wall of St. Peter on the Rock Episcopal Church honoring Gerald Blake. Both St. Peter's and the Murray Bay Protestant Church have other plaques memorializing its young sons, Harold Wrong and Gerald Blake. At the Murray Bay Protestant Church on August 10, 2014, on the hundredth anniversary of the beginning of the Great War, Archbishop Bruce Stavert of Quebec offered prayers for all those killed from that community in World War I, and red poppies filled the vases on the altar that would have been used in the summer of 1910. A member of the congregation said that one could feel the presence there of the young college students of such great promise who had sat in the pews 100 years before.

In 1977, at the age of 81, Constance Marani recalled other Murray Bay summers to an interviewer from the Havergal School Old Girls Association for alumnae of her preparatory school in Toronto:

"You went all the way from Montreal and slept on the boat. You went down past Quebec City and into every little village and wharf...and you could hear the French Canadians calling "*Haulez le slack la bas.*" The tides would be out and it would be way, way down, and they had to let the gangplank way down and you had to walk up a hill. If the tide was in, it would be all slimy and green and sea weedy, with that salty smell. The names were so intriguing...Les Eboulements, Ste. Irenee and Murray Bay. When you arrived there, the dock was very, very long. All along the wharf were the horses and carriages and hay carts for your luggage, waiting for your luggage, waiting for you. And it would be your private person, Henry or Honore or someone, and we all waved at each other. You would pile off with your 15 or 20 pieces of luggage and children.

"I wonder why we, and all those Americans, went so far. Some one person must have found it. Both Sam and Edward Blake adored sailing and they had yachts and they sailed. Sailing was almost unheard of on the St. Lawrence because of the currents and tides as well as the coldness of the water. You would be dead in minutes. Mother never let us go into a canoe, although we had one, and my brother wasn't allowed to use the sailboat after my father died. We had an 18-foot dingy at Murray Bay, right at the dock. He wasn't allowed to have it until he was 18 because his mother was so afraid of the water.

"The ladies dressed in long frilly petticoats and dresses on board the sailboats, little hats perched on their heads. There are pictures of my mother and grandfather with red and white striped stockings on at Murray Bay. We often rented a French house and the habitants moved out for the summer. They charged $100 a season with ice, wood and water. Of course, in the first few years the houses did not have electric lights or bathrooms. We went out to the barn or to the little outhouses. The ice house was one you walked into through two or three doors. The butcher came around with a cart and you did all your shopping right at your front door, butcher, fish and vegetables, that sort of thing.

"Mother took it for granted that we would speak French. We talked a very bad patois when we played with the French children."

CHAPTER FIVE

The Sedgwicks: Murray Bay Patricians

"Beyond Murray Bay there is only Heaven."

—Henry Dwight Sedgwick

For those who know of the notoriously glamorous Edie Sedgwick, forever linked with the movies she made for Andy Warhol and his 1960s "factory," it would be hard to imagine that the elegant Harry Sedgwick, known to his family as "Babbo" was her grandfather.

The great-grandfather of contemporary actress, Kyra Sedgwick, Harry Sedgwick died in 1957 at the age of 95. As a youth in Stockbridge, Massachusetts—the Sedgwick ancestral home—he had heard people running through the streets announcing that Abraham Lincoln had been shot. Just three years before he died he married Gabriella Ladd, a sculptor in her forties. His first wife May Minturn Sedgwick died in 1919, never having recovered from the death of two of their children.

Harry Dwight Sedgwick
Murray Bay Protestant Church collection

Marvelously dressed on every occasion, even for hiking into a private fishing camp, Harry Sedgwick personified the Harvard educated, New York bred patrician who came to Murray Bay and fell in love with everything. Although he and May traveled extensively with their children through France and Italy as Sedgwick researched Marcus Aurelius, Henry of Navarre, Lafayette, Dante and Madame Recamier, and other subjects of his extensive biographies, they rarely missed a summer in Murray Bay.

"The picnics were such a tradition. Someone would announce in the morning: Now is the time of year when we go to the....and off we would go on these expeditions—pilgrimages really, always to the same place year after year. The wicker picnic basket had to be brought down, the thermoses filled with syllabub, which was a kind of drink made of claret and milk.

"Eugene, the Canadian who worked for the Sedgwicks, would launch these two old town canoes. Babbo wore stockings that came up to his knickerbockers and folded over once and what he always called his Cinderella slippers. Eugene would go ahead of us in a little rowboat to clear the ground where we were to picnic. He was always dressed in a striped waistcoat, a white shirt, and a black tie over a celluloid collar.

"When we got to the island, we'd spread blankets and things would be brought from the canoes. The food was really marvelous—including thin sandwiches with cucumbers in them, and watercress and almost no mayonnaise and a little bit of butter and no crusts. Even the Sedgwick lemonade had to be made in a certain way. After the picnic, Babbo would always read aloud—P.G. Wodehouse was his absolute favorite. Sometimes he found something in the Letters of Marcus Aurelius and we were expected to commit it to memory (He never used the word memorize.) He would read for about half an hour and it would be getting dark by then and people would take turns holding the torch so that Babbo could continue the passage."

—Helen Burroughs Stern
Second wife of Harry Sedgwick

Sedgwick was quite close to his brother-in-law Isaac Newton Phelps Stokes, author of *The Iconography of New York*, who, of all the Minturn and Sedgwick relations, matched Babbo's description of himself as an Epicurean. Although he had studied law at Harvard and practiced for a short time in the prestigious New York firm of Beaman, Evarts, Choate at 52 Wall Street, he considered the law not to be his calling. "I was mentally and morally uncomfortable," he wrote. "As if I were swimming in glue."

Like his brother-in-law, Newton Phelps Stokes, and Newton's wife, Edith, he also responded strongly to the needs of the poor and didn't feel that the law responded to their needs. He tried several different jobs for a few years. His Minturn in-laws had been very involved in the founding of Brearley School for Girls in New York and Harry served as headmaster there for one year.

In addition to his writing and gardening for himself and Murray Bay friends, Sedgwick felt that appreciating life was his principal calling. "His real career was his life: the people, places and literature that filled it. He closed one of his letters to me, 'Squeeze the flask of life to the dregs,'" wrote his grandnephew Harry Sedgwick.

From his book *Memoirs of an Epicurean*, he writes: "All the world's a stage and men are not only actors, but spectators. They deem their roles important, serious, charged with heavy conse-quences...they shout, they huzzah.

"Epicureans are not like that. They regard themselves primarily as spectators and though they do not underrate the value of what used to be called Life's blessings—health, domestic affections, interest in one's work—and though they entertain a decent regard for the opinions of their neighbors, they set great store by their seats in the pit, and try to secure such as shall command a full view of the stage; they feel that in the long run the value of life depends upon one's interest in the human comedy, as it is oddly called—comic yes, but tragic, farcical, brutal, bloody."

Sedgwick turned to Epicurus whom he felt dreaded all manner of excess and who chose a garden as a place to teach and defined himself by this decision. To Henry Dwight Sedgwick, his garden in Murray Bay mirrored his life. Set close to the shore of the St. Lawrence River, the first Minturn house became known as the Sedgwick house. He wrote poetry about his flowers including "Ode to Pansies" in tribute to robust pansies that bloom all summer in Murray Bay, unlike pansies in gardens farther south.

Harry was the descendant of Judge Theodore Sedgwick who moved to Stockbridge, Massachusetts just after the Revolutionary War. Judge Sedgwick was a compatriot of Alexander Hamilton and George Washington. He and his wife Pamela appear in a painting depicting the first reception for Martha Washington as First Lady. The judge's descendants were almost all buried at the Sedgwick Pie in Stockbridge, visiting there frequently during their lifetimes.

Harry recalls being presented to writers Mark Twain and William Dean Howells, painter John La Farge, violinist Ignacy Jan Paderewski, and other celebrities at a time when he was a young attorney in New York, but it was poet Matthew Arnold, whom he met as a college student at his family's home in Stockbridge who most impressed him.

"He came to dine at my father's house and I did not dare to talk to him, but I feel still that it was an honor to have met him."

Harry's brother, Ellery Sedgwick, became editor of prestigious *Atlantic Monthly* in 1905. His daughter married author John P. Marquand, whose novel, *The Late George Apley*, centers on a graveyard much like the Sedgwick Pie.

Helen Burroughs Stern first came to Murray Bay as the new wife of Harry Sedgwick and recalled the Sedgwick house, built by Sarah Shaw Minturn, at a later date:

"The Murray Bay house was large, with porches, and an enormous green lawn leading down to the water. The water was just freezing cold. The days were like the water, shining and scintillating. The house contained the strangest combination: beautiful braided rugs were everywhere made in the local abbeys up there...glowing rooms with satiny walls and lovely lamps...and yet the lampshades were bought down at J.C. Penney's and they had Mickey Mouses on them. Suddenly you found things that were totally tasteless. The Sedgwicks just didn't care about that sort of thing."

"I am very eager for another summer in that dear place," Babbo wrote to a relative. "Beyond Murray Bay there is only heaven," Babbo wrote to a relative late in life when Murray Bay was a constant dream.

When Babbo died in 1957 he was buried in the Sedgwick Pie on a wintery day when snow lay pristine on the ground. His young wife, Gabrela, said to John P. Marquand, Jr: "I was saying to Babbo the other day, 'when you get to paradise you're going to leap, leap, and leap.' And perhaps he was hoping that it would look a good deal like his Murray Bay garden beside the St. Lawrence."

On August 20, 1910, Harry and May Sedgwick brought three of their children to the Murray Bay Protestant Church. They had been married in 1895 as had her sister Edith to Newton Phelps Stokes. At that time Babbo was Assistant District Attorney in New York, but due to a reversal in family fortune, he was living in a boarding house on East 22nd street. Although the Minturns had also endured major financial reversal due to unscrupulous dealings of a business partner of May's and Edith's father, they were able to maintain a compound of adjoining brownstones near Gramercy Park on 22nd Street as well as summer in Murray Bay.

On August 20, 1910, 14-year old Henry Dwight Sedgwick IV, nicknamed "Halla," 11-year old Minturn Sedgwick, and six-year old Frances Sedgwick would have been seated between Babbo and May and would have attended the Sunday school class taught by Supreme Court Justice and church warden John Marshall Harlan.

A daughter Edith, named for her beautiful aunt, had been born to Babbo and May nine years earlier and lived for just a day. The baby had been buried in Sedgwick Pie and her older brothers picked flowers in the rain for her grave.

Like her mother Susanna Shaw Minturn, who had lost three of her seven children, May Sedgwick struggled desperately with grief and depression. Like in the Sedgwick family, severe depression characterized many Minturn women. Minturn Sedgwick, later to be a Harvard football legend, was the strongest of the boys, probably idolized by both parents. At age eleven, Halla and his younger brother Minturn were delivered by their parents to a London boarding school called Bedales. May and Babbo took young Francis with them to Rome where Babbo was researching a book on Italy. Like his father and unlike his athletic brother Minturn, Halla was devoted to reading.

After two years, Halla was sent to Groton School in Groton, Massachusetts, and his brother Minturn joined him two years later. Founded by 27-year old Reverend Endicott Peabody in 1884, Groton was the beloved school of President Franklin Delano Roosevelt, who quoted Dr. Peabody in his fourth inaugural address, invited him to perform his wedding to his cousin Eleanor

Roosevelt, and often entertained him in the White House.

Called by *Time Magazine* the "Most Famed United States Headmaster of His Time," Peabody was the subject of Louis Auchincloss's best-selling novel of 1964, *The Rector of Justin*. A writer in the tradition of Edith Wharton, Auchincloss was one of the many famous Groton School graduates, as well as a cousin of Jacqueline Kennedy. The Headmaster's daughter, Helen, would one day marry Minturn Sedgwick. The Rector often summered in Murray Bay with his daughter Helen and her family, and worshiped at the Murray Bay Protestant Church. Peabody's descendants include actresses Edie and Kyra Sedgwick and model Penelope Tree.

Harry Sedgwick quoted Alice Roosevelt Longworth when he described his maternal grandfather as "a great slab of New England granite." Peabody produced a notable group of national leaders through what many referred to as "muscular Christianity." Peabody was actually rather suspicious of too much intellectual learning; his aim was to turn out enlightened public servants and Christian gentlemen."

Franklin Roosevelt often said that there was no one beyond his parents that he respected more than the Rector. The Rector often visited the White House during Roosevelt's presidency and it is reported that the president told a colleague when the Rector left: "You know, I am still scared of him!"

It was at Groton just four years after that sunny day in the Murray Bay Protestant Church that Babbo's and May's lives fell apart. For the athletic Minturn, Groton was forever a playing field. He joined the varsity football team and became the school's champion wrestler. For his older brother, Halla, an epicurean like Babbo in the making, who liked nothing better than committing to memory passages from *The Rubaiyat of Omar Khayyam*, Groton meant teasing from fellow students on occasion.

In the spring of 1914, just weeks before graduation, Halla and Minturn rowed together on the Nashua River and then raced on the mile long path back to school. The following day, Halla was admitted to infirmary with a fever and was diagnosed by the school doctor with pneumonia. Although the doctor felt it was nothing serious, May took a train from New York and his father followed.

In his privately printed book about Halla, "In Memoriam," Babbo wrote:

"That night we gathered by his bed, Minturn on one side, kneeling and holding his hand, their heads together. May and I sat on the other side, Ellery and Mr. Peabody at the foot. Mr. Peabody read from the prayer book and we repeated the daily prayers we always said with the boys. Toward morning a bird sang on the little tree beside his window, and then, as the day was dawning, his spirit left us. As I saw the coffin in the Groton chapel, Horatio's words burned themselves into me: "Good night, sweet prince, and flights of angels sing thee to thy rest."

Her other sons felt that May never recovered from the death of Halla. She wrote to her mother, Susanna, shortly after she lost her son, recalling the death of her own brother, Franciés Minturn:

"It is not until our own hearts are pierced that we can begin to know the suffering of others." May never recovered from her grief, suffering a series of strokes, and dying in 1919.

Minturn would wear his Groton nickname of "Duke" throughout his life. The *Boston Globe* headline, "Sedgwick Turns Tide" was something his proud father never forgot. Fans would never forget that he led the Harvard football team to Rose Bowl glory.

Francis would enter Groton in several years, but was slight of build and no match for his athletic brother. He suffered so greatly from the death of his mother that he was forced to leave Groton and his father placed him in the Cate School in Santa Barbara, California. Although he followed Duke to Harvard, he never found the same success. Just prior to the Great Depression, he took classes at the Harvard Business School which interested him not at all, and he was encouraged to develop his artistic side. At times volatile and mercurial, Francis was diagnosed as manic depressive and entered the Austin Riggs Clinic in Stockbridge, Massachusetts. Despite his emotional unrest, the beautiful socialite Alice de Forest married him in Grace Church in New York, in a ceremony performed by the Rev. Dr. Endicott Peabody, Headmaster of Groton.

Francis and Alice moved to California where they had eight children, the seventh child was Edie Sedgwick.

CHAPTER SIX

The Harlan and the Fish Families, and the Remarkable Mabel Boardman

Lives of Service

"I do not believe there is a more beautiful spot on God's earth," said U.S. Supreme Court Justice John Marshall Harlan, speaking about Murray Bay.

United States Supreme Court Justice John Marshall Harlan discovered Murray Bay in 1897, soon thereafter renting the legendary Maison Rouge, owned by the Honorable Edward Blake, member of the British Parliament.

In her book, *Some Memories of a Long Life*, first published by the Journal of Supreme Court History, Harlan's wife, Malvina, documents their Murray Bay days:

"In our rental cottage, set among the spruces on the cliffs overlooking the St. Lawrence we had 14 in residence, including children, grandchildren, and other family members. One friend said it was the funniest household he ever saw, that every time you turned around you met a mother-in-law."

As the wife of a Supreme Court justice, Malvina was quite accustomed to entertaining large groups. "Mondays" was the name of receptions given at their Washington homes by wives of Supreme Court Justices on that afternoon on a regular basis. Often 200-300 guests attended and a lavish buffet, including rich foods, light salads, and elaborate desserts, was expected. Musicians played, including members of the musically talented Harlan family.

Malvina was a close friend of First Lady Lucy Hayes, the wife of President Rutherford B. Hayes, who would be called "Lemonade Lucy" because of her strong temperance stance. Malvina served as a talented and elegant partner to her husband throughout their 53-year marriage. Wed on December 23, 1856 in her parents' home in Evanston, Indiana, Malvina and John moved to his home in Frankfort, Kentucky.

John Marshall Harlan, 1833-1911, was expected by his lawyer father to one day serve on his country's highest court, hence being named for Chief Justice John Marshall. When John Marshall Harlan took his oath of office on December 10, 1877, at age 44, he was the third youngest person to be named to the Court and would serve for almost 34 years, the third longest term at that time.

Justice Harlan played a role in some of the most important civil rights decisions of the time, including issuing the lone dissenting opinion in *Plessy v Ferguson*, the infamous case that endorsed separate, but equal segregation.

In memoirs later published in the Journal of Supreme Court History, Malvina Harlan, widow of Supreme Court Justice John Marshall Harlan, wrote about her Murray Bay memories:

"I think that the family of Mr. William Howard Taft began to spend summers there around 1895 when he was Chief Federal Judge in the Ohio circuit. Upon his return from the Philippines in 1904 or 1905, he resumed his place in our summer colony, greatly to the pleasure of his hosts of friends at Murray Bay."

In the summer of 1904, a surprise birthday party had been planned in his honor. Taft's birthday was celebrated by his growing clan and friends for years to come.

Malvina Harlan relates that the event began with a torch light parade of his men friends to a cottage where Judge Taft and his wife had been deployed in advance:

"One of the features of the evening was a dance in which Judge Taft, greatly to my surprise, asked me to join as his partner. I had heard how accomplished he was in that line and I said, 'Oh, you must excuse me, I have not danced in many,

many years and I could not at all interest or keep up with you as a dancer.' But he replied, 'It is only the Virginia Reel.' Looking around I saw my husband led out by Mrs. Taft to take the head of the line. Thinking to myself, 'Well if he can dance, I can.' I reconsidered the matter and quickly took my place with Mr. Taft at the end of the line.

"It was understood that no one under 40 should be eligible for the reel and we dancers had much fun to ourselves over the comparatively small number that were willing to confess to being over forty, although all looked on with longing eyes, while we old boys and girls renewed our youth. It was a most delightful and jolly occasion."

Taft had a much-deserved reputation as a dancer. During his days as Governor General of the Philippines, he had mastered the intricate national dance, the Rigadon. It was reportedly much easier for him because of Virginia Reels he led frequently in Murray Bay.

Very merry and musically talented, Malvina was one of the best chroniclers on early days in Murray Bay. Her book, *Some Memories* which dates from 1854 to the year 1911 when John died, was praised for its fine portraits by United States Supreme Court Justice Ruth Bader Ginsburg who writes in the introduction:

"Her manuscript was found among the justice's papers lodged at the Library of Congress and I was drawn to it as a chronicle of the times, as seen by a brave woman of the era. Malvina wrote of her adjustment as a 17-year-old bride, when she left the free state of Indiana in 1856 to reside with John and his parents in Kentucky, and of her feelings when her mother-in-law presented her, on arrival, with a personal slave. She strove to serve her husband selflessly, yet did not surrender all pursuits of her own, particularly the music that broadened her life. We learn of the extraordinary encouragement Malvina gave to her husband when he wrote the lone dissent from the Supreme Court's judgment striking down the civil rights act of 1895, a measure Congress enacted to promote equal treatment, without regard to race, in various public accommodations."

Writing on her decision to marry John, she comments: "All my kindred were strongly opposed to slavery. Indeed, my uncle was an out-and-out abolitionist that I think (before he came to know my husband) would have rather have seen me in my grave than have me marry a Southern man and go to live in the South."

When her husband decided to enlist in the Union Army, five years after their marriage and with two small children at home, she wrote, "Summoning all the courage I could muster, I said

Judy Carmack Bross

you must do as you would do if you had neither wife nor children. I could not stand between you and your duty to the country and be happy."

Malvina's book shows many examples of her as a wise wife. Justice Harlan collected American history memorabilia and he had been given the inkstand that Chief Justice Taney used when he penned the 1857 Dred Scott decision which held that no person descended from a slave could ever be a citizen and that the due process clause safeguarded the process of holding another person as a slave. It was a decision with which Harlan strongly disagreed and it was overturned later by the 14th Amendment.

Harlan had met a woman who claimed to be a relative of Taney and he chivalrously offered to give it to her. Malvina felt this was the wrong decision and hid the inkwell away and he had to tell the woman it was lost. The next day she polished the inkstand and removed all others from his desk. When her husband came home she told him that he "would find a bit of inspiration on his desk."

"The memory of the historic part that Taney's inkstand had played in the Dred Scott decision, in temporarily tightening the shackles of slavery...in the antebellum days, seemed that morning to act like magic in clarifying my husband's thoughts in regard to the law that had been intended [...] to protect the recently emancipated slaves in the enjoyment of equal 'civil rights'. His pen fairly flew on that day [...] he soon finished his dissent."

Malvina's book, authored four years after John's death, starts where it all began in the front parlor of her Evansville, Indiana home: "One day during the late summer of 1853 [...] a young girl of 15 peeped through the almost closed window-shutters and saw a young man passing by [...] she knew at once that he was a stranger. That was 61 years ago, but as clearly as if it were yesterday she can still see him as he looked that day—his magnificent figure, his head erect, his broad shoulders well thrown back—walking as if the whole world belonged to him."

At 9:00 in the evening on December 23, 1856, wedding guests gathered for a "tableau wedding," thought to be something very inventive for the times. The 14-member wedding party gathered in the closed back parlor and was arranged in a circle with the bride and groom in the center. The clergy and a few family members stood with them and when assembled, the doors were drawn and guests in the front parlor could appreciate the tableau and enjoy the ceremony.

John's rise from a country lawyer to national prominence was quick and the family moved to Washington, D.C. With her own merry personality and a close friendship like Nellie Taft with First

Lady Lucy Hayes, Malvina was a sought-after member of the Washington social circle. At one of her first White House dinners, she described Mrs. John Jacob Astor as being "fairly ablaze with diamonds." It is remembered that she wore over $800,000 worth of diamonds and was called the "Diamond Queen."

Malvina recalled that at that time ladies felt very comfortable in their black silk, probably the little black dress of the time, and with little jewelry. Not only did she attend grand balls at the White House, but dropped by the White House Green Room on the second floor on Sundays for hymn sings with her husband and the first family.

On the 25th anniversary of his term on the Supreme Court in 1902, Elihu Root, Secretary of War, and Philander Knox, Attorney General, gave a dinner in Harlan's honor. His former landlord, The Hon. Edward Blake, who was a member of Parliament in London, traveled to Washington, D.C. to speak at the dinner where President Theodore Roosevelt addressed the guests as well.

When the Supreme Court published Malvina's book in 2004—later to be published by Random House, her great-great-granddaughter, Kate Dillingham, a talented cellist, played at the launch party. A soloist who has played at Carnegie Hall as well as with the Moscow Symphony Orchestra and the St. Petersburg Philharmonic, Kate has continued Malvina's love of music. Kate said recently: "My great-great grandfather, Justice Harlan established the First Presbyterian Church in Washington D.C. on New York Avenue. I find it interesting that he was a deeply religious man, yet firmly committed to the separation of church and state. And everything I heard about Malvina convinces me that she was quite a force."

The Harlans' son Richard and his wife were the first family members to discover Murray Bay. They had spent the summer of 1896 there and insisted that their parents and Malvina come in June with her two daughters as "the advance guard" to investigate Maison Rouge, with her husband remaining behind for a series of lectures at the summer law school of the University of Virginia.

The Harlans took a three-year lease on Maison Rouge. Richard corresponded frequently with the Hon. Edward Blake who was, at that time, a member of the British parliament, representing one of the Irish constituencies.

A rare collection of Blake family letters from the late 1890s conveys details of the rental agreement of Maison Rouge. In May 1898, Gerald Blake, Edward's son who lived in Toronto, acknowledges the receipt of $212.50, the rent for the summer:

"If you will refer to Mr. Edward Blake's letter to yourself of the 11th October last, you will see that the bedding accommodation was there fully set out by him as follows—four double beds, nine single beds, three camp beds, ordinarily used as couches. This is the amount of bedding accommodation agreed upon for the house, and it seems to me a matter of small importance, to determine exactly which rooms the beds are in at this moment. They can no doubt be easily moved when you find what will be the most convenient distribution for you.

"I think that my father will have serious objections to any alterations in the structure of the building. It is possible that he might be willing to allow you to cut a door in the manner suggested, but I certainly could not assent to this arrangement without his express approval."

Richard Harlan was obviously trying to find the most room possible for a family more and more fond of summers in Murray Bay. Having been rented by so many of Murray Bay's first families, including the Minturns, Maison Rouge, with its many rooms and beautiful view of the St. Lawrence, was a prime property in the 1890s, sadly to burn down in the second decade of the new century.

The Harlans remained at Maison Rouge until 1902 when they built a cottage of their own on land adjoining Tamarack top, a house on the Boulevard which Richard's wife built in 1898 on what she described as a "beautifully wooded tract of land." Their other son, John Maynard Harlan, and his wife Elizabeth Palmer Flagg were the parents of the second Supreme Court Justice John Marshall Harlan II, who had long-term rental cottages for many summers in Murray Bay.

Malvina wrote of her house in Murray Bay: "The very location—a sunny meadow in the high bluff or brae—led me to call our permanent home "Braemead," a name that seemed natural to my Scotch-Irish blood which I inherited from my dear father. From its lovely verandahs, we could see the majestic St. Lawrence and the far off opposite shore, 16 miles in distance; the beautiful curve of the bay into which the Murray River empties; the beautiful profile of the picturesque Laurentian range to the north, purpling in the evening lights; and the spruce-clad nearer hills towering above us at the west. The Panorama in every direction gave us pictures of surpassing beauty, which no brush could ever rival or do justice to.

"My husband and I passed many hours together on the Braemead verandah, drinking in the beauties of the scene, often saying with a thrill of loving reverence in his voice as he thought of the giver of "every perfect gift"—"I do not believe there is a more beautiful spot on God's earth."

A Harlan family descendent still lives in Braemead, high on the Boulevard, surrounded by the magnificent pine trees Justice Harlan loved and many grandchildren play in front of that panoramic view.

Malvina wrote that the justice took a great interest in the French habitants. "Their ingenuity and their display of really skillful work in certain directions was a source of never-ending wonder to him."

For Justice Harlan, golf was a Murray Bay discovery.

"Shortly after his arrival, my son Richard persuaded his father to take up golf. It was a radical change in his habits of life, for up to that summer he had never indulged in any out-of-door diversion as a relief from the constant strain of professional labors. It proved to be a most healthful pastime for him, both mentally and physically. His love for the game grew upon him steadily and during the next fifteen summers which he spent in Murray Bay, his interest in it never flagged. Golf is the chief diversion among the main visitors to Murray Bay."

In the summer of 1906, when Taft took a two-month vacation with Nellie and the children in

Murray Bay, his assistant Archie Butts chronicled that he encountered Harlan on the Murray Bay golf course "jumping up and down to coax a ball in that was hovering on the very edge of the first hole." Seeing that his jumping wasn't working, he called out to the future president, "Come on! You jump. That will do the business."

Henry Dwight Sedgwick perhaps best captured Harlan's time in Murray Bay in "The country of the dormer-window" which appeared in *The Century* magazine in September 1913:

"The great charm of Murray Bay lies even more in the character and disposition of its people than in beautiful scenery. To everyone who has been long familiar with Murray Bay its most delicate charm lies in the memories of the men whose dignity of character and fine friendliness of manner set a special seal on this beautiful place. Among those who will not come again to brighten the summer days by their presence are Mr. Edward Blake and Mr. Justice Harlan. These men belonged to the history of Canada and to the history of the United States, but in matters that do not concern the muse of history, they belong to Murray Bay. No golfer can tee his ball without involuntarily expecting to see Judge Harlan's noble figure striding joyously from hole to hole, and to hear his exultant, boyish glee over a good stroke or his humorous explanation of an unlikely one. No worshipper at the Protestant church, that pretty stone church on the village street, could pass by without a glance to the spot where the justice used to stand on Sunday mornings, a symbol of large-hearted, Christian hospitality and to greet the congregation as it struggled in. Indeed, Murray Bay is rich in human memories that outdo nature in her prodigal attempts to make the place delightful."

Malvina's recollections of Murray Bay end with a memorial to her husband a year after his death:

"His Murray Bay friends arranged for a beautiful memorial of his devotion to the little union church and of his deep interest in the community as a whole (the habitants as well as the summer visitors). Over the main entrance to the church and facing the public road, they placed a fine 'Town Clock'. The hands and hour-numbers made of hammered Norwegian iron, painted black; and on the wall inside the church, near the main door, they placed a beautiful memorial brass tablet reading as follows:

To the honored memory
Of
John Marshall Harlan
1833-1911
A justice of the Supreme Court
Of the United States
For Many Years a Trustee of This Church
Soldier, Patriot, Christian
The Church Clock is Dedicated

* * * * *

MABEL BOARDMAN

"The Red Cross Is the great volunteer aid department of our country to administer the generosity of the people in time of national and international need." Murray Bay resident and Red Cross chair, Mabel Boardman in "Under the Red Cross flag at home and abroad."

From high above Murray Bay's most prestigious boulevard, the woman who succeeded Clara Barton as head of the Red Cross and created the complex service organization it is today, surveyed society. Mooring Lights, the gray-shingled cottage which she built with broad verandas able to accommodate several hundred for her famous teas, could be called Murray Bay's grandest home and Mabel Thorp Boardman, socialite, philanthropist, and change agent, would become its most illustrious Grand Dame.

Having presided over the Red Cross relief efforts following the San Francisco earthquake, the sinking of the Titanic, famine in China, and the St. Pierre volcanic eruption in Martinique, Miss Boardman was well-equipped to handle any social flutter that might occur in Murray Bay.

Mabel Boardman
Marianne and Bernard Pillet, private collection

Despite rather serious photographs, she was known as one of Murray Bay's great hostesses. The front of Mooring Lights was all ballroom with views to the wide St. Lawrence, offering square dancing and reels as Saturday night entertainment. She employed the Villeneuf family—the most celebrated family of French Canadian musicians— to be chauffeurs and other staff members and their music enchanted guests Saturday nights.

From a Juliet balcony from her second floor bedroom, one of seven on that floor, Miss Boardman welcomed her guests in calèches (and later snappy automobiles) who had climbed the steep hill after driving through her elaborate iron gates created in a nearby foundry. Deep purple clematis climbed the pillars by her front door as they still do today.

Guests proceeded to an enclosed veranda executed in a chinoiserie style with 10-foot tall oak doors opening onto her wide front lawns facing the St. Lawrence. The veranda was also used for frequent bridge parties. A double fireplace near the entry was used when an evening chill arrived. Carved into the shutters at most dormer windows in Murray Bay were signature symbols, such as the swallows at Les Hirondelles, hearts at the second Minturn cottage. Miss Boardman's many windows bore the formal French fleur de lis.

Because of their close friendship, rumors spread that perhaps there was more to the relationship between Miss Boardman and William Howard Taft who served as President of the Red Cross and advised Miss Boardman on many matters relating to international issues. In Doris Kearns Goodwin's *Bully Pulpit*, she writes:

"Born in Cleveland in 1860, the always-single Miss Boardman had a friendship with Taft all her life. The Tafts and Boardmans had moved in the same political and philanthropic circles in Ohio. That continued when the Boardmans moved to Washington, DC in 1888. Her father, William Jarvis Boardman, was a lawyer active in politics and was the grandson of Senator Elijah Boardman. Miss Boardman, like Justice Harlan, had learned of Murray Bay from William Howard Taft, and their friendship grew even stronger in Murray Bay. She was a favorite guest at the president's birthday party at the end of summer and he attended her dinner parties usually for 50 guests or more. Even in Murray Bay she sought out the advice of the man she most admired on her increasing Red Cross leadership."

Miss Boardman's Red Cross training made managing crowds easy and with the Villeneuf family as her staff, the meals she served featured the most delicious of Charlevoix's traditional dishes such as *tourtiere*, a pork and vegetable pie with pastry crusts as only the French Canadians can prepare. Leeks, fraises du bois (tiny alpine strawberries), hazelnuts, tiny blue plums and the tastiest of tomatoes found their way to her tables, and maple syrup appeared often as an accent to meats and cold soups. A *tarte au sucre* (sugar pie) would grace the dessert table, along with puddings in brown sugar sauce and apples picked from the nearby Isle-aux-Coudres.

Although she perhaps longed to be in Murray Bay and often took her series of Packard cars on the train with her so that a member of the Villeneuf family could meet her and get her to Mooring Lights as quickly as possible when the season began, Miss Boardman was regarded for her strong work ethic at the Red Cross.

Her desk at the new headquarters in the War Building in Washington, D.C. had just been placed following the Red Cross reorganization led by Miss Boardman when word arrived that the great San Francisco earthquake had occurred and that the city was in flames. Her job would not only involve marshaling nurses and relief workers, but raising huge amounts of funds for the city.

"For the first few days, millionaires and paupers stood side by side in the breadlines, but as rapidly as possible the abnormal breadlines were done away with and an army rations system was put into place," Miss Boardman wrote in her book,

Judy Carmack Bross

Under the Red Cross Flag at Home and Abroad,
"Relief was pushed through four broad channels:
food, then clothing, along with common household
necessities, then shelter and last, the means to
make one's own provision for the future."

If Florence Nightingale, founder of the
International Red Cross, will always be known as
"the Lady with the Lamp," Mabel Boardman might
be seen as "the lady with the flow chart and
checkbook" as well.

In her first ten years of service alone, Miss
Boardman directed relief efforts for over 75
disasters including earthquakes, fires, volcanic
eruptions, cyclones, famines epidemics, ship-
wrecks, and mine disasters. Although she relied on
strong board members and advisors such as
William Howard Taft, senior government and
military officials, financiers and social workers, it
was her insistence on schooled nurses, prevention
training, absolute organization, and community
coordination that transformed the American Red
Cross. Miss Boardman called for "organizational
humanitarianism" and expanded the Red Cross in
an increasingly professional way.

In June of 1900, the Red Cross had been re-
incorporated by an act of Congress and required to
provide financial statements annually. Following
the great Galveston, Texas hurricane that took
over 8,000 lives in September 1900, there was

serious disagreement over how money had been spent. Clara Barton had appeared almost immediately on the scene of what was called the greatest natural disaster in American history. Firsthand stories of survivors extolled her selfless efforts, but recordkeeping and staff training were not her strengths.

A committee composed of senators, congressmen and an army general came in to investigate and determined that an audit should take place. Some funds given to help in the Armenian famine as well as the Johnstown flood of 1890 were found to have been diverted to pay for lands in the west and a Red Cross park had been built.

Clara Barton, who had been the image of the organization, had much charisma, and personally took charge at all major disasters, was forced out in 1904 and Miss Boardman took charge. The old organization had been dissolved and a new corporation created by an act of Congress signed by President Theodore Roosevelt.

"The new charter provided that all accounts should be audited by the War Department and an annual report submitted to Congress by the Secretary of War," Miss Boardman wrote. "For the first time the American Red Cross became truly national in scope and standing."

Although she was the acknowledged leader of the American Red Cross, Miss Boardman refused to accept a title, feeling that people might question her experience. Although the President of the United States presided at the annual meeting, issued public appeals in war and disasters, and made board appointments, it was Miss Boardman who ran the organization. She considered that one of her most important acts had been to convince her close Murray Bay friend to serve as President of the Red Cross.

At the first annual meeting, William Howard Taft, then Secretary of War, was elected president and this office he continued to occupy by annual elections after he became president of the United States. In March 1913, on retiring from the presidency, he resigned as president of the Red Cross, giving his reasons in the following letter:

"I was elected president of the Red Cross in December to succeed myself. I had been president for four years during my incumbency as President of the United States. The cause which the Red Cross promotes is greatly aided, I think, by having the president of the United States as its head, and I do not think that it embarrasses the incumbent of the office of president of the nation to accept the office as head of the Red Cross."

President Wilson then accepted the job.

A tribute to President Taft noted in the *Red Cross* magazine:

"Only those who endured the strain of the early days of reorganization, who bore the burden of the many complex problems of development, who battled against discouragement and disappointments, can comprehend what the constant interest, the helpful, tireless counsel and the sympathetic inspiration of Mr. Taft's eight years' presidency meant to the Red Cross. He built foundations that are true and strong like the man himself, not counting the structure raised upon them for the credit of the man but for the service of his fellow man."

Until the end of his life, President Taft continued his friendship in Murray Bay with the remarkable humanitarian Mabel Boardman.

* * * *

HAMILTON FISH

"And when I die, you will find Murray Bay engraved on my heart," said Hamilton Fish IV in an address to the Canadian embassy late in his life, paraphrasing Mary Tudor who is alleged to have said: "when I die you will find Calais engraved on my heart."

Hamilton Fish III

In 1901, glamorous, notorious and perhaps the most famous architect of the opulent Gilded Age mansions, Stanford White, designed for the wealthy New York lawyer Alfred Clark Chapin the third commanding villa on the cape already occupied by the Minturn and Bonner/Cabot houses next to the Murray Bay Protestant Church.

Instead of a Newport mansion of the type he constructed for the Vanderbilts and Astors, White built an airy cottage with dormer windows and wide bays facing the rocky beach just below. The name "Bord d'Eau" was well chosen. It was destroyed when the Boulevard de Comporte was created to connect Pointe-au-pic with La Malbaie with a four-lane road, leaving just the Bonner and Minturn houses to tell of gracious life at the turn of the last century.

Choosing Stanford White as his architect signaled that Chapin wanted the very best. Although McKim, Mead, and White had designed the first Minturn house and other Murray Bay residences, Chapin was interested only in White. The famous architect had no formal training, but he had served as an assistant to Henry Hobson Richardson. Architect of major public and private buildings in America's major cities, Richardson contributed the "Richardson Romanesque" style seen in Trinity Church Boston, his masterpiece just blocks from the Augustus St. Gaudens memorial to Susanna Minturn's brother, Robert Gould Shaw, on the Boston Common.

An active salmon fisherman, Stanford White had explored the Restigouche region on the southern shore of the St. Lawrence. Realizing that the rivers of the north shore were also prime for salmon as well as trout perhaps encouraged him to take the project.

The year that he designed Chapin's house would be the year that triggered his downfall, leading to his murder by a jealous husband in 1906. In 1901, White met Evelyn Nesbitt. Just over ten years before, White had designed and built the second Madison Square Garden in New York City and created a tower apartment for himself where he could retreat to design in a quiet setting. It was also be the spot where he entertained very young chorus girls. From its tall ceiling hung the famous red velvet swing. Evelyn was not the first young woman White seduced there, but she was one of the youngest and most beautiful. In 1901, she was a standout in the Broadway musical, "The Floradora Girls," and quickly captured White's attention. The restaurant atop his Madison Square Garden hideout became the scene of his murder when Evelyn's millionaire husband, Harry Thaw, killed White in a jealous rage. The subsequent courtroom events would be called "the trial of the century" and has been the subject of many books and movies.

Alfred Clark Chapin, the wealthy New York lawyer who became mayor of Brooklyn in 1888, started a congressional political dynasty to be carried on for five generations when he was elected to the United States Congress in 1891. His descendants, beginning with his son-in-law, Hamilton Fish, filled the past century with their leadership.

Born in South Hadley, Massachusetts, into a family of prominent and wealthy New Englanders, Chapin graduated from Williams College and Harvard Law School. Chapin became New York

Railroad Commissioner after resigning from Congress in 1892.

Reading from his collection of rare books on the veranda of his villa delighted Chapin throughout the rest of his life. When they were children, Roland Martel, who currently lives in Murray Bay, recalls playing with the Fish children in the house before it was torn down. In a wide front room, he recalls seeing an enormous pool table with lion claw ball feet that had also brought delight to earlier generations of Chapins and Fishes.

Chapin had been in good health until the end of the summer of 1936 when he began to fade. He suffered a heart attack on September 10th, but rallied enough to go on to Montreal where he died on October 2nd at the age of 88. Chapin's second wife, the former Charlotte Storrs Montant, whom he married in 1913, was by his side.

It is remarkable the number of Murray Bay summer people who one could imagine willed their way through one last August sunset or bright September morning before they succumbed. Several of Murray Bay's most beloved residents, including Frank Cabot and Justice John Marshall Harlan, died in the fall following bittersweet last summers along the St. Lawrence.

Judy Carmack Bross

Chapin's first wife, Grace Stebbins, died in 1908. Her daughter Grace continued to accompany her father to Murray Bay. Previously married to William Beverly Rogers, Grace married Hamilton Fish III, a cousin of her first husband, in 1920.

The first Hamilton Fish, who was also the 16th Governor of New York, entered Congress in 1843. His grandson Hamilton Fish III, who lived to be 102, served in Congress from 1920 until 1945 and when he celebrated his 102nd birthday, he was the oldest living American to have served in Congress. His son, Hamilton Fish IV, died in 1996 after serving 13 terms in Congress. He was the member of the family who spent the most time in Murray Bay and is most remembered by the community.

The following story, told by Alex Paterson, longtime Murray Bay resident and family friend, captures poignant Murray Bay memories:

"Ham and his first wife, Julie, were very good friends of many French-speaking year around residents. Bertrand Villeneuf and his sons used to sing old songs of the Charlevoix at many of our picnics and the boys were Ham's friends, playing together in the summertime. When Julie died in a tragic automobile accident at a very young age, one of the Villeneufs travelled from Murray Bay to attend and despite the fact that he spoke no English, he rose in his pew at the end of the service and, unaccompanied, sang one of Julie's and

146

Ham's favorite Charlevoix songs. Emotion and raw courage permitted him to deliver what Julie and Ham would have wanted the most at that moment."

When Hamilton Fish IV died in 1996, a memorial service was held at the Cabot gardens. Les Quatre Vents, once again bringing together the families who lived nearby on the Murray Bay cape.

CHAPTER VII: LIVES OF FORTUNE

Ezra and Therese McCagg

"I would like this place simple, and yet I want the visitor or friend to be not conscious that there has been any artful thought in this arrangement but to say mentally how pleasing it is to the eye," wrote Ezra Butler McCagg in a letter to his landscape architect, Frederick Law Olmsted, Jr. in 1899 about his Murray Bay home on the old Quebec road, just above Maison Rouge.

"The Spinney" was designed by Charles McKim, head of McKim, Mead and White with a garden by the son and namesake of the legendary designer of Central Park and the grounds of the Chicago World's Fair and a close friend of Ezra McCagg. It was the second house to capture the heart of the Chicago philanthropist.

Substantial in size, colonial in appearance, and gracious in scale, the Spinney still offers a secluded and romantic corner for its residents and guests. The broad porch wraps around the handsome white clapboard cottage, original white wicker chairs and planters filled with pale lavender coreopsis remain to encourage guests to enjoy the view. The name "Spinney" means a copse, a setting in a glen. Surrounding Olmsted's English summer garden are pine, arbor vitae and birch trees, providing the feeling of a secret garden.

Ezra McCagg
Courtesy of Northwestern Memorial Hospital
Chicago, Illinois

To read a resume of Ezra McCagg would be to note the major institutions which made Chicago great. An eminent lawyer, McCagg was President of the Chicago Club and of the Board of Northwestern Memorial Hospital, trustee of the University of Chicago, a major funder of the art union which pre-dated the Art Institute and patron of the portrait painter, George P.A. Healy. He helped found the Chicago Historical Society, the Sanitary District, the YMCA, the Chicago Astronomical Society and numerous other organizations.

A great believer in public parks, he first brought Olmsted to Chicago in 1863 to share his vision for the numerous open spaces along the city's lakefront. Slight in stature and overwhelming in energy, McCagg tackled every challenge with vigor. He had been born near the Hudson River in Kinderhook, New York in 1825 and began practicing law in Chicago in 1847.

His Chicago house, where he lived with his first wife Caroline, sister of Chicago's first mayor and wealthiest resident, William Ogden, reflected both his financial success and his interests.

"Incredibly magnificent for the city" is how noted author Edgar Lee Masters described the mansion in *The Tale of Chicago* in 1933. Located on the near north side of Chicago, it commanded two city blocks. Two large conservatories held rare plants collected on his trips around the world. He shared rare species with gardeners creating nearby Lincoln Park. His library was described as "large and stately, with floor to ceiling books." His collection included rare early Jesuit writings and letters believed to be among the best in the world.

While the Spinney remains, looking remarkably as it did when McCagg created it, the Chicago mansion was lost forever on Sunday, October 8, 1871.

In *The Great Fire*, David Lowe writes: "Long before daylight there was nothing but burnt-out shells where hours before silver had gleamed, oriental carpets had muffled the footfall and carved rosewood furniture had graced the high parlors. The McCagg's large home and stables burned in a few minutes, remarkably the impressive conservatories remained."

Surprisingly, several plants and trees stayed green and one of the palms which he grew in hiw own conservatory still grows in the Lincoln Park conservatory. His invalid mother and sister were rescued by servants and all the family moved to the Ogden mansion which was remarkably spared.

For Ezra McCagg, the loss was extraordinary. He and his first wife, Caroline, had been traveling in Europe, enhancing their extraordinary art collection when he heard about the fire's destruction. When asked to take part in the rebuilding of Chicago that had become a boomtown in 1872, he wrote that he just didn't have the heart to be a part of the reconstruction. Although he gained in strength, he grieved about the fire for many years, but for the City of Chicago, McCagg remained a model of public service. It was written of him, "He represented our best aspirations, and his example and personality in a community of striking individuals, made him its most important individual influence. He was always eminently and impressively an American gentleman, standing for the best there is in American civilization."

When Ezra McCagg planned his next beloved home in Murray Bay, he felt he survived two great losses: First the death of his wife, and second, the loss of his great Chicago mansion.

He married the vibrant Therese Marie Davis of Cincinnati on September 8, 1891. Because her father was an invalid, the wedding was a small one. Ezra was 67, Therese was 37, born in 1856, two years after Ezra's marriage to Caroline. A Cincinnati social writer noted that their wedding at the elegant home of her parents on East Fourth Street was "the scene of the notable event which transformed Miss Therese Davis into Mrs. McCagg."

"The bride of yesterday has for so long been devoted to church and charitable work in connection with Christ Episcopal Church that the announcement of the engagement some time since, created a decided sensation among Society's four hundred, the groom is a Chicago lawyer and millionaire. The bride wore a trim traveling gown of gray cloth in a fine diagonal weave. No useless flipperies disturbed its severe simplicity, and she approached the altar with neither veil or bouquet."

Following the ceremony, the couple traveled to Vancouver and sailed to Japan for a three-month honeymoon.

Murray Bay has had a remarkable number of strong and often large women who etched their places in the always-intriguing history of its summer population. Therese was no exception. A photograph of Therese which still hangs on the Spinney wall shows a formidable woman of commanding character. She loved music, entertaining, and painting and would outlive her husband by 25 years.

It is unknown who introduced the McCaggs to Murray Bay, but the Cincinnati Taft connection probably was what brought them there. The host of Chicago parties for visiting presidents Hayes, van Buren and Grant—as well as other important figures of the day such as Ralph Waldo Emerson and William Cullen Bryant, McCagg could have met the future president through Chicago political connections as well.

McCagg was a cousin of Louis Comfort Tiffany whose stained glass window graces the Murray Bay Protestant Church, and of Louis' brother Charles, who owned property on the Boulevard at the time. McCagg's close friend, Robert Todd Lincoln, had encouraged his mother, Mary Todd Lincoln, to withdraw to Murray Bay for a time following his father's death because of the unique beauty of Murray Bay.

McCagg was a founder of the Jekyll Island club, one of the most exclusive resorts in the world, and would have told his fellow members about Murray Bay. Founded in 1886 on an island just off Brunswick, Georgia, it promptly became known as a millionaire haven, a winter Newport. In a 1904, *Munsey's* magazine article, it was described as "the richest, most exclusive and most inaccessible club in the world." Its membership roster, limited to 100 families, included Vanderbilts, Rockefellers, Astors and Pulitzers, with a Chicago membership second only to New York in size. Due to his work in the creation of Chicago's Lincoln Park, Ezra McCagg was named chair of the committee on landscape engineering.

The *New York Times* reported in 1886: "It is not intended to be a selfish and exclusive man's club. On the contrary, ladies will constitute an attractive element and will be freely admitted to the privileges shared by their husbands, such as fishing, riding, bathing and camping."

Murray Bay was perhaps a symbol of McCaggs' new life, one with "my wife, the pride of my life." As their marriage began, they would be building something new and beautiful together.

After her husband's death in 1907, Therese built a yellow structure with broad high windows close to the Spinney. To this day it bears the name "The Studio" and she often retired there to paint. The front porch looked out onto the Olmsted garden, with its bushes and flowers, just as the garden looked in a scrapbook from almost 115 years ago. The Studio is owned today by the artist, Reeve Schley, and his wife Georgie. Schley often paints from the porch looking out on the Olmsted garden.

The local legend is that Therese would occasionally meet former President Taft for a romantic afternoon in the Studio. With their Cincinnati connection they had certainly known one another for many years. The legend continues that they were both large of girth and enjoyed having that in common. A doubter might say that rumors were also murmured about the President and Mabel Boardman, who also was a large woman.

Fifty years after Therese's death, a case before the District of Columbia Court of Appeals brought to the public arena once more the art collecting genius of her husband Ezra. In 1917, Therese had made an indefinite loan, to the National Museum of American Art of the Smithsonian Institution, of "South American Landscape," a painting by Frederic Church, exhibited by her husband in Chicago's first art exposition in 1859. Her descendents sued to recover the painting.

The *Chicago Daily News* wrote about this show of art collected by wealthy citizens: "Striking down the thought that Chicago was entirely devoid of all taste and culture in art." It further pointed out that "only 25 years ago our city was just an Indian trading post." What would become the most prominent piece in the show would be "George Washington Crossing the Delaware" by Emanuel Gottlieb Leutz, which hangs in the Metropolitan Museum in the room adjacent to John Singer Sargent's portrait of Edith and Newton Phelps Stokes. This iconic painting fortunately had been sold prior to 1871 by its Chicago collector, Alexander White, and thus avoided being destroyed in the Chicago fire.

Also prominently featured in the exhibition was a painting called "A view of the Saguenay," the deep river off the St. Lawrence at Tadoussac where the McCaggs and the Tafts had a private fishing camp, close to Baie Eternite.

Coming from Kinderhook, New York on the Hudson River, McCagg must have had an early love of the Hudson River School, and he and his brother-in-law, William Ogden, collected not only Frederick Church, but Asher B. Durand and John Frederick Kensett. "South American View" was featured in that exhibit which would ultimately lead the way to the establishment of the Art Institute of Chicago. It is not known how it managed to escape the great Chicago fire.

The court ruled in favor of the descendants of Therese's siblings that the loan should be terminated and the trial court directed the Museum to return the paintings to the estate for distribution to the owners. This painting and "Mountain Scene" by Francoise Diday, were sold at auction by Christie's.

Therese and Ezra are buried in the Episcopal cemetery in Stockport, New York with other McCaggs. At the time of Ezra's death in August 1908, the Chicago Tribune wrote, noting that he was well into his eighties:

"He was one of those enthusiastic workers for the public good to whom the men of this day owe so much but of whose services they are often unmindful."

GEORGE BONNER

George Bonner
Musée de Charlevoix

"Charlevoix county is considered to be the Switzerland of Quebec. Here the granite mass of the Laurentians, clothed in the spruce and fir mantle of the boreal forest, meets the salt-water coastline for the first time and it is at its most dramatic." From *The Greater Perfection,* by Francis H. Cabot, designer of Les Quatre Vents, considered by many to be the finest garden in North America.

Only three homes stood on the prominent cape overlooking the St. Lawrence and across to the Laurentians. Each would fit the definition of a magnificent summer villa with wide verandas and garden full of white hydrangeas as big as balloons. Two powerful families, the Cabots and the Fishes, joined Susanna Minturn, building two houses on the promontory occupied by the Murray Bay Protestant Church. The Cabots would create what is considered the most entrancing garden in North America. The Fish family would be called the United States Congress's most powerful dynasty, for five generations an unbeatable chain.

The homes of George Bonner, who was described by Helen Taft Manning as the richest man in Murray Bay, and Alfred Chapin, the wealthy mayor of Brooklyn, New York, were built in 1898 and 1901 respectively. Both men played an active role in the beginnings of the summer colony and of the Murray Bay Golf Club. Alfred Chapin's daughter Grace married Hamilton Fish.

George Bonner's Pointe-au-Pic home, later known as *Le Barachois* (a coastal lagoon protected by a sandbar) faces the St. Lawrence with graceful lines and a veranda sweeping around it. A recent owner has restored much of the character of Bonner's day. Described as a "kind, upright, successful man of business" by Henry Dwight Sedgwick in *Memoirs of An Epicurean,*" Bonner made his most important purchase, the Seigneury of Mount Murray in 1902. It is there that his great-grandson, Frank Cabot, and his wife Anne created the famous garden Les Quatre Vents, visited each summer by passionate lovers of gardens and beauty from around the world. Born in 1837, Bonner first visited the area when his family fled from the cholera epidemic of 1842, and his love of the surroundings as a five year-old never left him. He imparted that love to his descendants.

Maud Bonner Cabot and sons
Musée de Charlevoix

Today his great-great grandson, Colin Cabot, and his wife Paula, a talented opera singer, welcome guests to this magical garden filled with delphiniums over eight feet tall, rare blue poppies from the Himalayas, alleys of Lombardy poplars, and a Japanese garden praised for its serenity and harmony, among many other plants and settings.

One can imagine the magic of walking along the beach at the turn of the last century. Old paths close to the point where the Murray Bay River (now called the La Malbaie River) joins the St. Lawrence River added to the fascination of the property. There were farms the French would have tilled from the beginning of the 18th century. Bread ovens shaped like beehives, now standing abandoned between the larches and white birches, would have been fired every day, and as they still do, snow geese would have lingered on the Cabot beach, headed each spring and fall from the fields of Maryland and Delaware up to the Arctic Circle and back again.

The Bonners had immigrated to Canada from a small town close to Durham, England in 1820, settling in Quebec where his father developed a successful timber business. As a small child, George stayed in a little home on a beach farm that was built in the 1780s by the Seigneur Malcolm Fraser.

In return for the promise that they would be willing to go to Nouvelle France to colonize a cold, uncertain place, Louis XIV gave favorite soldiers and others large tracts of land called Seigneuries. At the time of the English conquest of New France in 1758, the town of La Malbaie was burned by the English on their way to attack the citadel in Quebec. General Murray, who survived the battle on the Plains of Abraham where the victor General Wolf died, divided the Seigneury into two pieces, with the southern side going to John Nairne and the other 90-square-mile parcel going to Lieutenant Malcolm Fraser.

"As a note—history of the name—Murray Bay. After the battle of Quebec, General James Murray gave seigneuries to two Scottish lieutenants. The names given to these two seigneuries were 'Mount Murray' (Cap a l'Aigle) and 'Murray's Bay' (La Malbaie). Murray's Bay devolved in usage to Murray Bay, but this is still an English name overlayed onto the local French names of villages. This is amazingly parallelled by the modern expansion of La Malbaie to incorporate so many local villages in order to simplify and reduce community expenses. (I think that Tim Porteus' introduction to Michel Choquette's record, 'Sur La Cote: Songs of Murray Bay,' 1959, best captured the concept of Murray Bay—what is the 'real' Murray Bay?)"

Shortly after his graduation from Kingston College, George left Canada for New York to join his brother John, who would later edit *Harper's* magazine. Beginning as an errand boy in a chemist's shop there at the age of sixteen, he went on to head his own stock brokerage firm with major financial ties to France. He married Isabel Sewell of Quebec, daughter of one of that city's most prominent families, and they had three daughters, Maud, Mabel, and Isabel. With Murray Bay never far from his mind, he retired at forty and spent much of the rest of his life salmon fishing in the Gaspe. At the end of the 1890s, he made a bid to acquire the island of Anticosti near the mouth of the St. Lawrence, known for its salmon. Having lost this bid, by chance he ran into his childhood friend, John Fraser Reeve, at the bar of the Garrison Club in Quebec. Reeve told him that the Seigneury was his for a price. Being in poor health, Reeve was happy to sell it to George Bonner for $50,000.

Bonner gave the Seigneury to Maud, then married to Francis Higginson Cabot. Her grandson, Francis, wrote that she was "for 50 years the spirit of the place." Called "Mootsie" by all, she was full of spirit and leadership. Bonner sold off a large portion with proceeds going to his other daughters.

Although the manor house and Les Quatre Vents were damaged by earthquake and destroyed by fire at different times, Le Barachois still stands proudly on the cape next to the second Minturn house, looking remarkably as it did when George Bonner built it. Le Barachois has changed hands several times, but one recent owner devoted great effort to restore it as it once was just after the house reached its 100th birthday. The houses not only have names in Murray Bay, but several have had centennial birthday celebrations. Auguste Choquette, a retired lawyer now living in Murray Bay, recalls spending the summer of 1945 in the house, then rented by his uncle. Age twelve at the time, Choquette remembered women in hats and veils at afternoon teas at the house and being told by his mother, "You better behave."

"We came into the port on a bateau blanc and I can still remember the salty but clean air and the wide rooms which faced the river at Le Barachois. There were always big events at Pointe-a-Pic."

* * * *

THE CAMAC FAMILY

"We had just come into the lounge of the Excelsior in Naples after dinner one evening and were sitting down to coffee and cigarettes when who should literally drop out of the clear blue sky but Miss Harriet Camac, whom we had known so pleasantly in New York and most recently in Rome, where with her mother she had passed the winter. She told us she had left Karachi six days before and would be in London 'day after tomorrow.' She was, and now she tells her friends about her air journey so delightfully and so matter of factly that it makes the old sea-way route seem almost like a cruise with Noah." Henry Prather Fletcher, former American Ambassador to Italy wrote in *From India to England by Air* 1929 by Harriet J.M. Camac.

"Oh, that Harriet Camac" is a phrase several longtime Murray Bay residents remember their parents uttering. Like so many summer Murray Bay matrons, Harriet addressed the world with determination.

"It was the way my mother drew out the last name when she said it that made me wonder," one second-generation resident said. Being a beautiful strawberry blonde who appeared in a silent movie in 1924 and was pictured driving a Bugatti, contributed to the lore. But Harriet had had a secret that few might have guessed, one discovered over 113 years after her birth.

Wealthy Pittsburg doctor, Charles Nicoll Banker Camac built a three-story house for his wife, Julia Augusta Metcalfe, high on the Boulevard circa 1895. Later called "Shangri la," the house had 18 rooms—six bedrooms, four large foyers and five bathrooms. The arrival of their two daughters, Harriet, born in 1901, and Eva, born in 1903, centered their summers in Murray Bay and the family became very involved in the Murray Bay Protestant Church where Harriet and her husband were active later in her life. But in her 20s, Harriet took on the world with relish.

As the ambassador observed about Harriet, when she made up her mind about something, nothing would stop her. Before she traveled from India to England by plane, she had made the silent movie *The Iron Horse* in 1924, been painted in 1928 by a European artist as part of a series entitled the "15 most beautiful women in America," broken off her engagement to a handsome Bostonian Herbert Ellis Harrington in 1922, and met an aviator who was the secret love of her life.

Although Harriet doesn't appear in the credits for John Ford's *The Iron Horse*, considered by many his silent film masterpiece, she would have considered filming the epic about the coming of the transcontinental railroad up to her sense of adventure. Ford, the iconic director of western movies, felt that if this film—which he said later was his favorite of all he made—was about pioneers, the cast should rough it during shooting. Filmed on location in Arizona, Nevada, and New Mexico, the cast lived in boxcars throughout.

The trip to India was possibly an escape for Harriet after dealing with a painful secret.

She wrote: "After several months' travel in the Orient, the prospect of a long sea voyage to the United States was not enticing. I had heard much of the recently established air route from India to England. On making application at the Bombay agency for Imperial Airways, I learned that the passage from India to Persia, which was not brought up to standards set by the management, was not thought suitable for women passengers."

After presenting herself in person at the main office in Karachi, Harriet got a seat on the plane. After eight days of actual flying, Harriet had been transported over 5,000 miles in four planes—a journey that would have taken two to three weeks. Photos in the tiny book show a handsome pilot, Jimmy Alger, as well as exotic spots along the way.

The telling of Harriet's secret in full belongs to Maryse Cote, who bought Shangri La in 2013 and soon discovered in the basement trunks filled with

Harriet's souvenirs from around the world as well as photographs, clothing, jewelry, and letters.

In 1936, Harriet had married John E. Elmendorf and her father had sold her the Murray Bay house for one dollar. The Elmendorfs would later live in Bogota, Columbia where he worked as a bacteriologist to find a cure for yellow fever but would return to Murray Bay whenever possible. Harriet would die of cancer in February of 1972 and she, her husband, and her parents are remembered by a plaque in the church.

To Maryse Cote, the trunks told a fascinating story, and she took many hours to catalogue what she had discovered.

"In March of 2014 I had a distinct impression that I was supposed to look at the photographs on the wall and turn them over. I was particularly drawn to a photograph of a little girl in what would have been Harriet's bedroom. The house was so charming, we had not wanted to change a thing. When I turned the photograph over there was a puzzling message. Earlier I found many photographs of a tall and handsome pilot whose name wasn't attached, and photographs of Harriet in loose clothes looking very pregnant as she set sail for England where she remained for several months with her mother. The photograph of the little girl looked blonde like Harriet as a child."

Maryse found the photograph on Sunday, March 30th before returning early the next morning to her home in Quebec City, carrying one box of photographs and planning to display the trunks filled with the rare souvenirs at the Musée de Charlevoix. On Tuesday, April 1st, the house burned to the ground. Sadly, as with many old Murray Bay villas, an electrical short probably caused the fire.

"I can't help but think I had found something Harriet didn't want anyone to find," Maryse said. "She wanted to keep that secret."

CHAPTER EIGHT

Murray Bay in Literature
John Rathbone Oliver

"Of all the places I've been in, I have never known one quite like this. Other places I've always been willing to leave—glad to leave sometimes. But I've never wanted to go away from here. I've always wanted to stay longer."

Henry Randolph addresses his sister Anne in *Rock and Sand*, John Rathbone Oliver's novel about Murray Bay.

Several early travel writers reported on the excitement of taking a white ship and landing at the Pointe-au-Pic dock, then being ferried to a hotel at the top of the hill in a calèche. The American writer, William Dean Howells, described in his novel, *A Chance Acquaintance,* the impression of a passenger upon pulling up to the Murray Bay dock in 1873 after having visited Quebec City:

"Further down the river from Quebec we had seen along the river shore looking bright and populous villages of habitants clustering about its slim-spired church. Soon we saw hills in the distance and a much-galleried hotel proclaimed a resort of fashion in what seemed to be a wilderness. Indian huts stretched with birch bark nestled at the foot of the rocks. I imagine that the visitors to the resort feel a fashionable desolation when the boats depart."

Of all the authors writing about Murray Bay at the turn of the last century, John Rathbone Oliver best captured the lives of the rock, which he considered the habitants to be, and sand, the Americans who came as summer visitors. An Episcopal priest, boarding school master, physician, and psychiatrist, Oliver first visited Murray Bay in 1894 and returned every summer for many years. In 1899, he helped build by hand the tiny Anglican church, St. Anne-In-The-Fields, which stood at the head of the Boulevard where it met the Quebec road, not far from the homes of the Harlans, McCaggs, and Blakes, and knew Gilded Age Murray Bay by heart. His own house was just off the Boulevard near the church that he built. He focused on what he called the two threads—the Americans and French Canadians—which were necessarily woven together.

It is the Americans who go away to grand homes in New York, Pittsburgh, Cincinnati and Chicago, from October to June wrapped up in their lives far from Charlevoix. One of Oliver's characters best describes the Murray Bay life is forgotten by the Americans when they return home in the fall.

"You know, Anne, there is something peculiar about this place. I come up here every summer and I've almost forgotten the names of the people that were such intimate friends of mine ten months ago. But after I have been with them for a few days— why they sort of grow into my life again and it seems as if I were going to stay here with them always. Then autumn comes, I have to go, and leaving is like pulling teeth. But pretty soon I forget about them—and the whole queer thing starts again," Robin Randolph muses in *Rock and Sand.*

Contrasted is the character of Amayas, an orphan raised in a Catholic orphanage in La Malbaie, who, as a young man caddied for Anne Randolph and expressed his devotion in many ways, including saving her cottage from intruders in the midst of a Murray Bay winter. His thoughts for Anne throughout the year were devotional, not romantic. Thoughts of Anne took him through the terrible winters.

It is the habitants who stay to face the almost six months of winter. "For when the snow came down and when the side-wheeler steamboat from Quebec stopped running, then the villages were cut off completely from what we often miscall civilization.... In the small villages themselves, there were small stores. The owners often became the arbiters of life and death, for they kept on hand small supplies of groceries and of tinned stuff...and they gave credit. By the middle of the winter the villagers had spent all their little ready money. Many of them then counted the days until the summer visitors came again, so that they might earn enough by renting their houses, their calèches or their horses, to pay off their debt to the storekeepers.

"Early in the autumn, long after the last summer guest had gone, most of the villagers and all the farmers banked up the lower stories of their wooden houses with earth and fallen leaves. This lower story was hermetically sealed for the whole winter and the family lived on the upper floor, every window of which was fastened tight and every crack or cranny stuffed with bits of old cloth. No breath of air from the outside air got into those upper rooms for more than six months of the year...people went hungry too in those winters. In some parts of French Canada, on the outlying farms, people go hungry still."

Some of the stronger men worked in logging camps. The Hearst newspapers and other chains obtained all their pulp paper for East Coast papers from the area. Boys earned a little money taking supplies to them. If the winter went too long, food for the horses and cows would be no more and the animals would die of starvation. How could the habitant family earn any money if they could not sell milk to the summer visitors or pull them in the calèches?

It is American families such as the Harlans, Tafts, and Cabots whose lives were most enriched because they, like Oliver, were greatly impressed by the spirit, talents, and work ethic of the French Canadians and took time to get to know them in a deep way.

Mary Louise and George Dixon
Musée de Charlevoix

The Dixons, good friends of the Tafts, chronicled Murray Bay summers in treasured photo albums.

POSTSCRIPT

Trouble:
Postcards from Mid-Century Murray Bay

"Today's resort old-timers believe firmly in a curious theory of resorts. This theory is that, generally speaking, the following groups have come to the social resorts in this order: first, artists and writers in search of good scenery and solitude; second, professors and clergymen and other so-called "solid people" with long vacations in search of the simple life; third, "nice millionaires" in search of a good place for their children to lead the simple life (as lived by "solid people"); fourth, "naughty millionaires" who wished to associate socially with "nice millionaires," but who built million-dollar cottages and million-dollar clubs, dressed up for dinner, gave balls and utterly destroyed the simple life; and fifth, trouble."

—Cleveland Amory
The Last Resorts (1948)

The private diaries of one mid-century Murray Bay doyenne are locked in the Canadian national archives, not to be opened for another 60 years. They are rumored to contain secrets of the Boulevard too hot to handle in her day and yearned to be learned by those who remember Fern Culver, the glamorous keeper of the diary. Possibly they tell of the true nature of the relationship between Canadian Prime Minister Mackenzie King and Beatrix Henderson Robb, whose home, Les Falaises, was considered by many to be the most beautiful house on the Boulevard. King, the liberal Prime Minister from the 1920s until the 1940s, who served more terms than any other Canadian prime minister, kept secret his use of mediums to stay in touch with departed associates and his mother. It was said by someone who knew her when he was a young man in Murray Bay that Beatrix Robb knew what she wanted and the Prime Minister was her frequent visitor when he wanted to get out of Ottawa. When one of the several Blake Boulevard houses burned down, she was there before the ashes died with an offer to build her dream house using her son, Boston architect, J. Hampden Robb, to execute a villa in the style of a Norman chateau. Mr. Robb later told the current owner that working for his mother wasn't easy.

Perhaps the diaries reveal the contents of a hidden room in a cottage along the Boulevard owned by another Canadian government official containing marked money and lurid letters as has been hinted.

The story of East German call girl and alleged Soviet spy, Gerda Munsinger, and Murray Bay Boulevard resident and Canadian Cabinet minister, Pierre Sevigny, was international knowledge, the subject of a movie and songs by two Canadian bands. Termed Canada's first sex scandal in 1966, it was paired forever in people's minds with the John Profumo and Christine Keeler affair in London. Sevigny, who had lost a leg in the war, brought Gerda to his large Charles Warren cottage several times, according to local lore, when his imposing wife was not around. The glamorous blonde was the daughter of a Communist Party worker. She immigrated to Montreal in 1955 and worked at various times as a waitress, call girl, and nightclub hostess. She aspired to be a model.

Under pressure from Prime Minister John Diefenbaker, Sevigny ended his affair with Munsinger and resigned from the cabinet in 1963. The Sevigny house was sold soon after.

Icons of Andy Warhol's factory days, Edie Sedgwick and Brigit Berlin, spent childhood summers in Murray Bay before their white hot careers defined what Warhol defined the "15 minutes of fame" that celebrities were often given. In a *Vogue* magazine article of 1965 under a heading "What people are talking about:

Judy Carmack Bross

"Youthquakers," Edie was described as a Sixties throwback to her cousin, Gertrude Minturn, an "I don't care girl" making movies for Warhol, sleeping with Mick Jagger, unforgettable with her "White hair contrasting with her anthracite black eyes, legs to swoon over, in a long black leotard." Like Gertrude, Edie died young, not of suicide, but of drug abuse.

Richard Berlin and his wife, Honey, lived in Sur Le Mer, one of Murray Bay's largest cottages, hidden away down a long road and overlooking the St. Lawrence. The Berlin children, Brigit and Richie, spent their summers at the Manoir Richelieu Hotel and are remembered. A friend of her children described Honey as a "New York socialite who slept until noon and had a dressing table with enough products to equip Bergdorf's make-up counters." She is also remembered regarding her constant hounding of her daughters to lose weight

It is fortunate that descendants of Boulevard residents know many stories and unsealing the legendary diary is not the only way to learn more. Gerda, Edie, and more from Mid-Century Murray Bay will help tell the unfolding story of this halcyon and adventurous spot in another Murray Bay volume.

ACKNOWLEDGMENTS

Many people say that Paris is their second and spiritual home. Not me. When my husband John Bross and I first visited Murray Bay ten years ago, the heroes from the past immediately presented themselves and I knew I had found my spiritual home.

First, we compiled the "People behind the Plaques" at the Murray Bay Protestant Church, a title that our history committee gave to notebook histories we developed on the Tafts, Harlans, Minturns, McKays, and so many more. My husband and the other Church Trustees encouraged this historical project and Virginius Hall, former head of the Richmond, Virginia Historical Society, did fine research and headed the committee. I realized that the air of Murray Bay was not only the freshest anywhere, but alive with history.

I thank my husband, John Bross, for his assistance with proof reading and suggestions for this work.

Judy Carmack Bross

Being the daughter of the newspaper editor, George Carmack, and his writer and photographer wife, Bonnie Carmack, I knew I had to tell it. The archives of the Murray Bay Protestant Church have helped me greatly in telling the stories. My three children, George York, Charlotte Matthews, and Alice York remind me so much of my parents in terms of their fine qualities and accomplishments. I thank them for encouraging me to write—they are my inspiration.

And, Willow and Sedgwick, our Abysinnian cats, served as my delightful mewses.

Celebrating Murray Bay with my extended and beloved new family, Suzette and Ally Bulley, Jonathan Bross, Lisette Bross and Ray Caccioli, Dolly and Jack Geary, and Aaron House, makes summer sublime. Sharing magical Murray Bay moments with grandchildren Addison, Allan, Avery, Clara, Colin, Daphne, Eloise, Henry, Hilary, Lucy, Oliver, and Parker is just the best.

I am most grateful to Carol Zimmerman of The von Raesfeld Agency in Henderson, Nevada, who served as my editor and advisor. Her work is outstanding and very supportive. I have great appreciation for Dorothy Hardy who designed a perfect cover using my vision of a Murray Bay summer visitor in 1910.

180

There are four present day heroes for me whom I thank enormously for the generosity of their help and richness of their information about Murray Bay.

Annie Breton, Director Generale of the Musée de Charlevoix in Murray Bay, gave me full and frequent access to their enormous collection of rare materials. The photo on the cover of this book reminds me of the beautiful and spirited Annie.

Louise Dempsey McKean, from a prominent French and American family, not only took a winter to translate our notebooks into French in memory of her childhood friend, Penny Cole, who died at age 20, but also shared all the important stories of Murray throughout the last century.

Tommy Hoopes, a craftsman and enthusiastic son of old Murray Bay, is the expert on Charles Warren and so many more residents. His collection of old Charlevoix postcards, William Hume Blake materials, and particularly his own memories, have been tremendously helpful.

Elisabeth Bacque is the best example of an extremely accurate and amazingly informed historian who shared iconic photographs and private letters with great joy.

I am grateful to Newton P.S. Merrill, grandson of Isaac Newton Phelps Stokes and his wife, Edith Minturn, for sharing his memories of his grandfather with me. The Phelps Stokes were not only glamorous and intriguing, but cared deeply for settlement house residents and others in great need.

Edith de Montebello and her niece, Kate Dillingham, descendants of Malvina Harlan, led me to materials on one of the most impressive women I researched. How proud she would have been of the accomplishments of Edith and Kate. I think they are like her because she did so much for the public good.

One of Canada's most celebrated leaders, former McGill University Board Chair, Alex Paterson, never failed to share a wonderful story and particularly fine memories of the Fish Family.

Maryse Cote, whose house Shangri La burned down in April 2014, shared her fascination with Harriet Camac, its former owner. Although so many of the house's treasures were destroyed in the fire, Maryse is not only re-building the house with her husband, Charles Angers, but is planning to write a book about Harriet. I thank her for all the intriguing information she shared about the Camacs.

Frederick Law Olmsted expert, Victoria Ranney shared private letters with me, discussing his work with the McCagg family.

Peter and Diana Taft, Cynthia Ryan, Sally Muspratt, Harvey and Kathy Sloane, Mary Jane Bancroft, Anne Douglas, Tisha Beaton, Roger Thomas, Brahm and Marilyn Elkin, Franny Van Dyke, Daniele Amyot—all honor their ancestors who loved Murray Bay and they have been inspirations as well as fine sources of information on the area.

Mac McKay, descendant of the legendary early minister, Alexander McKay, and a superior architect, made the life on the St. Lawrence come alive.

Marianne and Bernard Pillet were generous to share photos and information on Mabel Boardman.

Magdelon Monast is just as glamorous as was the former resident of La Folie Rose, Rose Tiffany. Many thanks to her.

I celebrate current residents, Angela Lancaster and Chuck Muckenfus, Georgie and Reeve Schley, and Lise and Daniel Tremblay, who recreate in their historic Murray Bay homes the magic of early day Murray Bay.

Two others have been inspirations for me as I wrote: Simone Clark, the wise, considerate and well-informed Murray Bay hostess whose distinguished husband Brock was a business leader in Canada, and Frank Cabot, who before his death told us fascinating stories about the Bonners, the

Judy Carmack Bross

Higginsons, and many early residents at his home at Les Quatre Vents.

My *Classic Chicago Online Magazine* business partner, Megan McKinney, author of *The Magnificent Medills* offered encouragement, advice, and books from her early Chicago library.

Milos Stehlik, Director of Facets Multi Media, kept checking to see if I was on track, saying, "There is a movie here."

No one could have helped me with more kindness and enthusiasm than Ethan Cotton and George Lesniak at Sir Speedy in Chicago, friends for years who tackled frequent book challenges with gusto.

I think Hamilton Fish IV said it for me..."And when I die, you will find Murray Bay engraved upon my heart."

NOTES AND SOURCES

Interviews with descendants of those present at the Murray Bay Protestant Church on August 20, 1910, the church archives themselves, and materials from the Musée de Charlevoix, the New York Historical Society, the Chicago History Museum, and the Newberry Library have greatly benefitted my research. Private letters, papers, and photographs shared by Elisabeth Bacque, Tommy Hoopes, Mayse Cote, Marianne and Bernard Pillet, and others have given me rare insight into daily life in Murray Bay at the turn of the last century.

Iconic Murray Bay authors, William Hume Blake and John Rathbone Oliver captured the relationships between Americans, French Canadians, the Scots, and the English. I am also indebted to early travel writers whose books and articles gave me the feeling of stepping off a bateau blanc at the Pointe-au-Pic dock for the first time.

I have also drawn on many family memoirs, such as those of the Minturn, Sedgwick, and Taft families and the widely respected *Two Centuries at Murray Bay* by Philippe Dube, amazing in its research.

Chapter One: Introduction

Mildred Minturn: A Biography by Leslie Minturn Alison, *Love, Fiercely* by Jean Zimmerman, and *The Loveliest Woman in America* by Bibi Gaston, supplied beautiful glimpses into the remarkable Minturn sisters and their families.

Reading the mimeographed "Random Reflections of a Happy Life" by Isaac Newton Phelps Stokes at the New York Historical Society not only provided me with a picture of the Stokes family and the courtship of Newton and Edith, but led me to the belief that these were truly exemplary people who focused on others in their work at settlement houses and other causes for the good of the community.

Edith Wharton's *Age of Innocence* set me in the midst of the Gilded Age and personal letters of the Blakes, supplied by Elisabeth Baque, and Helen Taft Manning's "History of the Tafts in Murray Bay," a talk she gave at a family anniversary celebration gave me an insight into Murray Bay at the turn of the last century.

Chapter Two: The Minturns

My major source in this chapter was a mimeographed autobiography of Isaac Newton Phelps Stokes which I read with great delight in the New York Historical Society. At the Society, I also read many newspaper accounts of Gilded Age weddings and social events.

Speaking with his grandson, Newton P.S. Merrill, greatly enhanced my enormous respect for this great historian of New York who published between 1915 and 1928 *The Iconography of the City of New York*, an amazingly researched history beginning in the sixteenth century.

Murray Bay Protestant Church archives and The Chicago History Museum told more about the Shaw and Minturn families. *Love Fiercely* by Jean Zimmerman, Leslie Minturn Alison's *Mildred Minturn: A Biography*, and Bibi Gaston's *Loveliest Woman in America* furnished fascinating accounts of the lives of the Minturn women. I am particularly grateful to Newton P.S. Merrill, grandson of Edith and Newton, for his personal insight.

Chapter Three: The Tafts

Peter Taft, grandson of the President, provided Helen Taft Manning's private history of the Tafts in Murray Bay, a spirited talk filled with memories and songs she read at several family celebrations.

The Bully Pulpit, Theodore Roosevelt, William Howard Taft and the Golden Age of Journalism by Pulitzer Prize winning author Doris Kearns Goodwin gave a fine glimpse of Nellie Taft's accomplishments and the couple's life before the White House.

The Autobiography of Malvina Harlan describes with great lightheartedness summer days with the Tafts in Murray Bay. As in all chapters, Philippe Dube's "Two Centuries at Murray Bay" was essential.

* * * *

Chapter Four: The Blakes

Elisabeth Bacque, a descendant of the Hon. Edward Blake and his wife, Ethel, provided the private correspondence of Constance Marani, the poems of Harold Wrong, a firsthand report on the November 2014 celebration of the life of Gerald Blake and many family photographs. Her careful insistence on accuracy and history have provided much help to other members of her family writing about its many accomplishments.

William Hume Blake enthusiast and scholar Tommy Hoopes gave me Blake's private letters on sailing the St. Lawrence, photographs and private correspondence. Records of the Murray Bay Protestant Church where William Hume Blake is buried were very useful as well. Blake's own summing up of the feelings in the fall when one leaves Murray Bay will always speak for the summer residents who must head home.

* * * *

Chapter Five: The Sedgwicks

The papers and books of Henry Dwight Sedgwick set the tone of the chapter, his elegance and his literary abilities had a lasting influence on Murray Bay. John Sedgwick's "In My Blood" described the depression which challenged so many members of this family. "Edie: An American Biography" by Jean Stein was very useful in reporting family impressions.

* * * *

Chapter Six: The Harlans. The Fishes, and Miss Boardman.

Malvina Harlan's book provided a fine glimpse into the dancing and golfing days of Justice Harlan and President Taft and revealed Malvina to be a modern woman whose traits of good humor and intelligence are mirrored in her descendants, Edith DeMontebello and Kate Dillingham, who I much enjoyed talking with about Malvina.

Reminisces of Canadian diplomat and University chancellor Alex Paterson gave me an insight into the Fish family and Mabel Boardman's "Under the Red Cross Flag at Home and Abroad" told of the growth of that organizations and the disasters they faced at the crucial time of Boardman's leadership.

Marianne and Bernard Pillet took me on a tour of Mooring Lights that they now own and showed me the beautiful iron gate which once led to her home, wonderful original photographs, and other treasures dating from her time in Murray Bay.

* * * *

Chapter Seven: George Bonner, Charles Camac and Ezra McCagg

Personal recollections enhanced my research as well as the many books on Chicago history which detailed the role of Ezra McCagg in building the city pre-Fire.

The papers of Frederick Law Olmsted, shared by Victoria Ranney, added information about his love of nature and gardening.

Conversations with the legendary Frank Cabot about his family as well as his marvelous book, "A Greater Perfection" told me more about George Bonner and the Seigneury.

I am indebted to Maryse Cote, who is planning to chronicle the life of Harriet Camac, for sharing her extensive research into the life of this intriguing woman.

* * * *

Chapter 8: Literature and Lore

Simone Clark introduced me to the works of John Rathbone Oliver who chronicled the lives of the Habitants of Murray Bay.

* * * *

Postcard Postscripts

Louise Dempsey McKean, Tisha Beaton, Tommy Hoopes, thank you for sharing your knowledge of Murray Bay legends. I look forward to further research for a sequel to this book.

UNPUBLISHED SOURCES

Blake, William Hume.

Marani, Ethel Constance. Interview with Buffy Evans Meredith for the Havegal Old Girls Association, 1977.

Olmsted, Frederick Law. Private Papers.

Phelps Stokes, Isaac Newton.
Random recollections of a happy life.
Mimeographed. New York Public Library, 1941.

* * * *

PUBLISHED WORKS

Alison, Leslie Minturn. *Mildred Minturn:
A Biography.*
Ste-Anne-de-Bellevue, Quebec: Shoreline, 1995.

Amory, Cleveland. *The Last Resorts.*
New York: The Curtis Publishing Company (1948).

Armstrong, Julian. *A Taste of Quebec.*
Toronto: MacMillan of Canada (1990).

Boardman, Mabel Thorpe. *Under the Red Cross Flag at Home and Abroad.*
Philadelphia: J.B. Lippincott Company (1915).

Blake, William Hume. *Brown Waters.*
Toronto: The MacMillan Company of Canada, Ltd., at St. Martin's House (1915).

Blake, Wlliam Hume. *In a fishing country.*
Toronto: The MacMillan Company of Canada, Ltd.,
at St. Martin's House (1922).

Bluestone, Daniel. *Constructing Chicago.*
New Haven, CT: Yale University Press, (1991).

Brinley, Gordon. *Away to Quebec: A Gay Journey to the Province.*
New York: Dodd, Mead & Company (1937).

Cabot, Francis H. *The Greater Perfection: The Story of the Gardens at Les Quatre Vents.*
Cold Spring Harbor: The Hortus Press (2001).

Camac, Harriet, J.M. *From India to England by Air.*
New York: Privately printed (1929).

Chatfield-Taylor, H.C. *Cities of Many Men.*
Boston: Houghton Mifflin (1925).

Cook, Frederick Francis, *Bygone days in Chicago.*
Chicago: A.C. McClurg (1910).

Culver, David M. *Recollections of a Lucky Life.*
Montreal: McGill-Queen's University Press (2014).
Dube, Philippe. *Charlevoix: Two centuries at Murray Bay.*
Quebec: McGill-Queen's University Press (1990).

Farr, Finis. *Chicago: A Personal History of America's Most American City.*
New Rochelle, NY: Arlington House (1973).

Fish, Hamilton. *Memoir of an American Patriot.* Washington, D.C: Regnery Gateway, 1991.

Goodwin, Doris Kearns. *The Bully Pulpit: Theodore Roosevelt, William Howard Taft and the Golden Age of Journalism.* New York: Simon & Schuster, 2013.

Grant, Bruce. *Fight for a City.* Chicago: for the Union League Club, 1955.

Harpster, Jack. *The Railroad Tycoon Who Built Chicago: A Biography of William B. Ogden.* Carbondale: Southern Illinois University Press, 2009.

Harlan, Malvina Shanklin. *Some Memories of a Long Life, 1854-1911.* New York: Random House, 2001, and originally, Washington, D.C., The Journal of Supreme Court History, 2001.

Howells, William D. *A Chance Acquaintance.* New York: Grosset & Dunlap, 1873.

Janher, Frederic Cople. *The Urban Establishment.* Urbana: University of Illinois Press, 1982.

Maloney, Cathy Jean. *Chicago Gardens: The Early History.* Chicago: The University of Chicago Press.

Marquis, Albert Nelson. *The Book of Chicagoans.* Chicago: A.N. Marquis. 1911.

Masters, Edgar Lee. *The Tale of Chicago.* New York: Putnam Sons, 1933.

Oliver, John Rathbone. *Four Square: The story of Fourfold Life.* New York: The MacMillan Company, 1929.

Oliver, John Rathbone. *Rock and Sand.* New York: The MacMillan Company, 1930.

Pierce, Betsy Love. *A History of Chicago: 1848-1871.* Chicago: University of Chicago Press, 1913.

Pratte, France Gagnon. *Le Manoir Richelieu: The Castle on the Cliff.* Quebec: Editions Continuite, 2003.

Schull, Joseph: *Edward Blake: Leader in Exile.* Toronto: MacMillan of Canada, 1976.

Sedgwick, Henry Dwight. *Memoirs of an Epicurean.* New York: The Bobbs-Merrill Company, 1942.

Sedgwick, John. *In My Blood: Six generations of madness and desire in an American family.* New York: Harper Perennial, 2007.

Simms, Florence Mary. *Etoffe du pays: Lower St. Lawrence Sketches.*
New York: The Musson Book Company. Ltd. (91)

Smith, Henry Justin. *Chicago's Great Century. 1833- 1933.*
Chicago: Consolidated Publishers, Inc. 1933.

Smith, Jori. *Charlevoix County, 1930.*
Quebec: Penumbra Press, 1998.

Stein, Jean. *Edie: An American Biography.*
New York: Dell Publishing Co., 1982.

Stemple, Antonia J. *Wharton, Edith, The Custom of the Country.*
New York: Charles Scribner's Sons, 1913.

Wharton, Edith. *The House of Mirth.*
New York: Charles Scribner's Sons, 1905.

Zimmerman, Jean. *Love, fiercely.*
Boston: Houghton Mifflin Harcourt, 2012.

ABOUT THE AUTHOR

The daughter of award-winning journalists, Judy Carmack Bross is a former newspaper reporter in Houston and Boston and a magazine writer in Chicago. She is co-founder of Classic Chicago, an online magazine to be launched in October 2015. In Murray Bay, she is the historian of the Murray Bay Protestant Church and the organizer of social history tours for the Musée de Charlevoix. She is a lifelong volunteer, currently working with the homeless in Chicago and with a Mayan community in Chiapas, México.

John and Judy Bross
Misión Surf, Tapachula, México

INDEX OF PHOTOGRAPHS

INDEX OF PHOTOGRAPHS

INDEX

CPSIA information can be obtained at www.ICGtesting.com
Printed in the USA
BVOW05s2100240615

406095BV00002B/59/P

9 781511 647922